LITERATURF
LITERATUI
THE CHI
400 S
CHIC.

D0083009

DATE		
4/98		

women's gothic and romantic fiction

American Popular Culture
Series Editor: *M. Thomas Inge*

Film: A Reference Guide
Robert A. Armour

women's gothic and romantic fiction

A REFERENCE GUIDE

Kay Mussell

American Popular Culture

GREENWOOD PRESS

WESTPORT, CONNECTICUT • LONDON, ENGLAND

Library of Congress Cataloging in Publication Data

Mussell, Kay.
  Women's gothic and romantic fiction.

  (American popular culture ISSN 0193-6859)
  Bibliography: p.
  Includes index.
  1. American fiction—Women authors—History and
criticism—Abstracts. 2. Bibliography—Bibliography—
American fiction. 3. Women in literature—Handbooks,
manuals, etc. 4. Gothic revival (Literature)
5. Romanticism. 6. Women and literature. 7. Women in
popular culture—United States. 8. Literary research.
  I. Title.   I. Series.
  PS374.W6M8   813'.085'09   80-28683
  ISBN 0-313-21402-6 (lib. bdg.)

Library of Congress Catalog Card Number: 80-28683
ISBN: 0-313-21402-6
ISSN: 0193-6859

First published in 1981

Greenwood Press
A division of Congressional Information Service, Inc.
88 Post Road West, Westport, Connecticut 06881

Printed in the United States of America

10 9 8 7 6 5 4 3 2 1

Copyright Acknowledgment

Permission to reprint from Dashiell Hammett, *The Maltese Falcon*,
in *The Novels of Dashiell Hammett*, © 1966 by Alfred A. Knopf, Inc.,
has been kindly granted by Alfred A. Knopf, Inc.

For my father

Contents

Introduction

Scholarly studies of popular culture materials have notably expanded in the past decade our knowledge of the American cultural past. By drawing upon such ephemeral material as pulp magazines, post cards, popular songs, children's stories, scrapbooks, films, and radio scripts and tapes, researchers have given us new insights into the leisure life of ordinary American citizens analogous to the insights being supplied by the new social historians and demographers. Much of this work is identification, retrieval, and preservation of objects that might once have been discarded as insignificant. However, in some areas of popular culture, enough material is now available to support substantial scholarly works of criticism and theory. The most highly developed area of popular culture knowledge is in popular fiction; this is true in part because books, and even some magazines, are more routinely preserved by libraries and individuals than are other materials. Books have a special value in the assessment of our cultural heritage and are less likely to be thoughtlessly destroyed. Among types of popular books, however, some have evoked more serious consideration than others. Perhaps the most thoroughly studied formula, to date, is the detective story, probably because it is a form that attracts intellectual and literate readers. Some of the finest criticism of the detective story has been written by scholars mulling over their own lifetimes' reading habits. Another formula of popular fiction that has been considered from a scholarly perspective is the Western. A number of writers on the

American experience of the West and expansion and on American themes of individuality and self-expression have found in pulp Western fiction a rich source. Science fiction also has its serious devotees, who gather in workshops, seminars, and institutes to discuss the genre and who publish essays and books on the topic. However, not all forms of popular fiction have been so fortunate as these, and among those relatively neglected formulas are the various kinds of fiction appealing primarily to women readers.

Because women's culture is conventionally perceived—(if it is considered at all)—as something apart from mainstream American culture, and because women as a group have been routinely ignored in much scholarly work, few scholars have taken an interest in the materials of popular culture that appeal specifically to women. In addition, women's fiction has suffered from insufficient critical attention in comparison to other formulas because women lack the access to outlets of expression and the legitimacy as subjects necessary to provoke scholarly controversy and study. Even after a decade of rich research and stimulating controversy about the experience of women in America, we know relatively little about their daily lives and about their hopes, aspirations, values, and world view. We are just beginning to be aware of the vast amount of resource material available for study of women in the past; and many of us are regretfully aware of the greater number of sources that have been destroyed. What remains often sheds an indirect and oblique light upon the topic and requires substantial and careful interpretation. Women's fiction is one of those resources.

This volume is a guide to research on two broad and overlapping types of women's fiction: the gothic and the romantic. Because of the relatively undeveloped state of scholarly study of these forms, I prefer to cast a wide net, leaving the fine critical delineations for later when the primary materials will be more accessible for analysis than they currently are. In this context, the definitions of gothic and romantic fiction are simply stated, revolving around the traditional role of women in culture. Both of these overlapping formulas of fiction address conventional women's concerns, although in slightly different ways. Both posit similar fictional worlds, although the significant elements upon which they concentrate differ to some extent. If gothic and romantic fiction are placed upon a continuum, the gothic novels would represent the more adventurous end and the romantic novels, the more domestic. In the world of gothic fiction, danger often threatens in the form of a villain; in that of romantic fiction, obstacles to happiness are more often of the characters' own making. In the nineteenth century in America, the gothic novel might be represented best by the work of Mrs. E. D. E. N. Southworth; the romantic, by Maria Susanna Cummins's *The Lamplighter* (1854). In the twentieth century, gothic novels by Phyllis Whitney, such as *Window on the Square* (1962) and *The Glass Flame* (1978), contrast similarly with any of the hundreds of Harlequin Romances popular over the past few years among American women and other English-speaking women around the world.

The world of the gothic novel offers vicarious danger and romantic fantasy of a type that is particularly appealing to female readers. Women are cast as victims in a man's world, but through the demonstration of feminine virtues, the victim proves herself worthy of salvation through the love of the hero, who becomes her deliverer from the terrors that beset her. The gothic villain, on the other hand, is capable of manipulating terrifying props and producing fear and danger, but he or she is defeated by true love. The gothic world view is supported by a highly particular set of conventions. Most stories are set in a remote place or time that lends itself to the complete intertwining of a terrifying mystery with a successful love story. Unlike the detective story, the gothic novel does not provide a logical solution to the mystery. On the contrary, the mystery and the love story are so coincidentally interconnected that it is virtually impossible to separate them. The solution of the mystery and unmasking of the villain usually remove the impediments to the romance. Women in these books are doubly victimized: by their feminine powerlessness and by their location in a place (castle, monastery, crumbling mansion, remote island) where a gothic villain can threaten them. The novels depend upon a setting in which the social order is hierarchical; the conventions of gothic fiction, such as mysterious inheritances, hidden identities, lost wills, family secrets, inherited curses, incest, and illegitimacy, require a world in which social mobility occurs through family identity and marriage rather than through individual success. They also depend upon the audience's belief that the culmination of courtship in the marriage of the main characters is the most satisfactory conclusion for the plot, thus elevating the place of family formation through love to supremacy.

Romantic fiction, on the other hand, is more simply a love story within a domestic drama, without the equal emphasis upon adventure and mystery. The romantic novel features a woman who experiences love, courtship, and usually marriage. Typically, it takes one of two forms: the drama of courtship and marriage within a setting of domestic detail, or the story of an already-achieved marriage with difficulties between husband and wife being resolved at the end, and the wife rewarded with either a better marriage to her current husband or a new marriage with a new lover. There are some romantic novels, also, of the "antiromance" type that tend to reinforce the assumptions of the form. These are novels in which the value structure and world view are unchanged, but in which the heroine behaves in such a way that she cannot be rewarded with marriage in the end. These, too, are romances, although the inversion of the plot makes them serve as cautionary tales rather than as models to be emulated.

The story of a romantic novel begins with an assumption, unquestioned and unexamined except in a few books, that the necessary, preordained, and basic goal of any woman is to achieve a satisfying, mature, and all-fulfilling marriage. The primacy of romantic love in defining a woman's place in the world and her personal and moral worth is rarely in doubt in these books. Their plots are often diffuse and may deal with many aspects of women's lives, but they never lose sight of that goal. Although other kinds of events and actions by the protagonist may take up much of the novel, they are always related eventually to the woman's marital status and condition of romantic happiness at the end of the book. The set of conventions for romantic novels is less specific than that of gothic novels, but they always relate to internal, domestic problems. Love relationships may be impeded by the heroine's immaturity, by the hero's stiff-necked pride, by the machinations of family members who wish to keep lovers apart, by the scheming of women who rival the heroine for the attention of the hero, by existing impediments to a marriage (wives, husbands, embarrassing earlier lovers who refuse to relinquish their hold on the heroines), and, most of all, by misunderstandings between the potential lovers that must be resolved before they may admit their love for each other. Occasionally, outside events intervene between lovers, although most women's fiction is notably apolitical. Even in historical gothics and romances, most events outside the domestic circle are significant only as impediments to the cohesion of domestic relationships. This is true even in Margaret Mitchell's *Gone With the Wind* (1936), a book in which most of the action has to do with Scarlett O'Hara's experiences during the Civil War and Reconstruction. The underlying value structure of the book is prescribed by Scarlett's relationships with men and, especially, by the contrast between Scarlett and Melanie Wilkes. In scene after scene, Scarlett responds to outside events as though they were mere disruptions of her personal happiness. In two other immensely popular antiromances, Susanna Rowson's *Charlotte Temple* (1791) and Kathleen Winsor's *Forever Amber* (1944), the protagonists are denied true love as punishment for their promiscuity. On the other hand, Maria Susanna Cummins's *The Lamplighter* traces the childhood and young adulthood of its main character, Gertie, showing how she learned to be a worthy and moral young woman through the influence of various other characters on her life; the novel confirms her virtue at the end by allowing her to marry the young hero, who has seemed through most of the book to be merely a friend to Gertie while attracted to another, and richer, young woman.

There is no question that love relationships are an important element of many different kinds of novels, although they are less significant in the formulas that appeal primarily to men, such as the hard-boiled detective story, the Western, or the spy thriller. It is difficult to imagine fans of James Bond, the Lone Ranger, or Philip Marlowe who would be satisfied with a book that ends with the hero settling down in blissful domesticity with the woman of the moment. The one novel in which James Bond is married, *On Her Majesty's Secret Service* (1963), ends with the murder by sniper of his new wife, just as they set off on their honeymoon. Bond could hardly reappear in the next book in his series encumbered with a wife; that would change the formula so drastically as to render it virtually unworkable. The same pattern applies to the heroes of Westerns and hard-boiled detective stories. In fact, one of the primary distinctions between men's and women's value systems in their popular fiction is stated explicitly at the end of Dashiell Hammett's *The Maltese Falcon* (1929) when Sam Spade explains at some length to Brigid O'Shaughnessy why he is going to turn her in to the police for her murder of his partner, even though he loves her. Spade's reasons would be incomprehensible to characters in women's romances.

"You'll never understand me, but I'll try once more and then we'll give it up. Listen. When a man's partner is killed he's supposed to do someting about it. It doesn't make any difference what you thought of him. He was your partner and you're supposed to do something about it. Then it happens we were in the detective business. Well, when one of your organization gets killed it's bad business to let the killer get away with it. It's bad all around—bad for that one organization, bad for every detective everywhere. Third, I'm a detective and expecting me to run criminals down and then let them go free is like asking a dog to catch a rabbit and let it go. It can be done, all right, and sometimes it is done, but it's not the natural thing. . . . Fourth, no matter what I wanted to do now it would be absolutely impossible for me to let you go without having myself dragged to the gallows with the others. Next, I've no reason in God's world to think I can trust you and if I did this and got away with it you'd have something on me that you could use whenever you happened to want to. That's five of them. The sixth would be that, since I've also got something on you, I couldn't be sure you wouldn't decide to shoot a hole in *me* some day. Seventh, I don't like the idea of thinking that there might be one chance in a hundred that you'd played me for a sucker. And eighth—but that's enough. All those on one side. Maybe some of them are unimportant. I won't argue about that. But look at the number of them. Now on the other side we've got what? All we've got is the fact that maybe you love me and maybe I love you."[1]

Such a passage from one of the prototypical novels in a predominantly male form contrasts with the world view of women's romantic fiction in several notable ways. In its reliance upon the logical listing and weighing of rational reasons, it contrasts markedly with the more emotional and instinctive decision making of women's novels. Some women's romances completely reverse the process when the protagonist, explaining why she chooses one lover over another, says that all the rational reasons would argue for a different choice, but she will follow her heart. Spade's commitment to his profession and to the external and internal values inherent in it is markedly different from the domestic orientation of female protagonists in women's novels. These women routinely give up their lives in the outside world as soon as they can do so with security. Spade's questions about whether his love for Brigid is strong enough to outweigh the other reasons are more fully articulated and much less subject to resolution than those in women's novels, where the questions are always definitively and easily answered in the last pages. Spade is unwilling to entrust his future to Brigid and that forces him into a series of decisions that send her to prison and keep him solitary and uncommitted. Women protagonists always find someone with whom they may successfully spend the rest of their lives (except in antiromances) and to whom they may commit without anxiety their future security, identity, and experience.

In women's romances, the love relationship has primacy over all other values and events. In a sense, it completes the significant phase of a woman's life and assigns her (presumably) to never-ending bliss for the rest of her life. Conventional family life, however, has no intrinsic interest for writers and readers of fiction because there is no suspense in it. In effect, women's romances imply that the excitement in women's lives ends in early adulthood, once they have completed the great quest for a mate who defines the rest of the forty or fifty years they will probably live. It would be dangerous, however, to underestimate the significance of this pattern, no matter how ludicrous it may seem, for in gothic and romantic fiction this great adventure is exquisitely exciting, overwhelmingly significant, and full of dangers and pitfalls that point to the inherent precariousness of women's lives. The achievement of a successful marriage is so important in the world of women's fiction that the two possible endings of such novels are polar opposites in absolute terms. A woman who wins her way through the obstacles, of whatever type, wins the ultimate value of being chosen as a wife; all else in her life may be anticlimactic, but at least it holds out the promise of being "good." Individual women do not reappear in subsequent novels since there are no adventures left for them, and a repetition of the love plot would be inappropriate. On the other hand, if a woman fails too fully, she may be consigned to an equally absolute oblivion, punished for her sins and forever barred from a successful rematch. Unlike James Bond, who always gets another assignment carrying with it the promise of another beautiful woman as his reward for success, a woman protagonist has only one task and, usually, only one chance. The endings of several antiromances illustrate the point. *Charlotte Temple*, one of the earliest of the American seduction stories derivative of Samuel Richardson's *Clarissa Harlowe* (1747-48), features a young woman seduced and abandoned in the New World. Her only recourse is to die. Although Margaret Mitchell leaves open a slight hope at the end of *Gone With the Wind* that Scarlett and Rhett may find each other again, Scarlett's "I'll think about that in the morning," might just as easily be further evidence of her characteristic indomitability. Rhett's final statement—"Frankly, Scarlett, I don't give a damn"—indicates the unlikelihood of reconciliation. In Kathleen Winsor's *Forever Amber*, Amber's true love rejects her for a final time and she goes on, presumably, to other promiscuous adventures, but the foreclosing of her possibilities for marriage and happiness is firm. Each of these women has stepped over the bounds of propriety and, for such breaches of the code, there is little forgiveness.

In the past few years, a new kind of gothic romance has become prominent in America. Perhaps the most descriptive term for them is "erotic gothic," for they combine the adventures, mysteries, and dangers of gothic fiction with quasi-specific sexual encounters. Most of these novels are paperback originals; publishers often market them more aggressively than many other women's romances, and their proliferation would indicate that the audience is now more tolerant of sexual adventure than it was in the past. However, these books also reinforce the conventional value system since most of them end with a happy marriage, and, in a significant number of them, many of the premarital— rarely, extramarital—sexual encounters (and there are many of them throughout these very long books) are not promiscuous since they are between the two lovers and sometimes under coercion. There are usually mitigating circumstances even when the protagonist has multiple partners. Therefore, these women are only superficially compromised and can still appropriately marry their lovers in the end.

Over the past two centuries, a vast quantity of romantic fiction has been written, published, and read in America and Britain, but much of it is elusive and not readily available. The most popular single works have long publishing histories and astronomical sales figures: Susanna Rowson's *Charlotte Temple* (1791), Maria Susanna Cummins's *The Lamplighter* (1854), Augusta Jane Evans Wilson's *St. Elmo* (1867), Mary Johnston's *To Have and To Hold* (1900), Margaret Mitchell's *Gone With the Wind* (1936), Kathleen Winsor's *Forever Amber* (1944), and Anya Seton's *The Winthrop Woman* (1958) all remained in print for many years after their initial publication. These most popular novels appeared on bestseller lists, occasionally were reviewed, and were taken seriously by readers and critics in their own times. But the mass of women's popular romantic fiction was, and is, truly ephemeral. Like pulp detective or Western novels, these thousands of books were read primarily by devotees of the formula or of particular authors. They have been the staple of circulating and public libraries since the eighteenth century, and for the past two decades their paperback sales alone make them worthy of consideration.

The most basic problem for the researcher, however, is to find the novels, in order to be able to assess the scope and character of these books over a very long period of time. Standard bibliographic sources, if they list gothic and romantic fiction at all, rarely if ever identify them as such; there is no standard source specifically listing these titles or authors. Often it is difficult to find the works in order to judge their content; this is especially true of nineteenth-century dime novel and story paper examples. Even hardback books are published, read, go out of favor, and languish on library shelves, unannotated and unremembered. Some of the great research collections, particularly of nineteenth-century material, are uncatalogued and require long hours of drudgery merely to determine if women's romances are represented in any significant numbers.

Problems of definition have also plagued this field of study, since its terms are so ambiguous. The terms *gothic* and *romance* do not lend themselves to consistent application. In its earliest British version, Horace Walpole's *Castle of Otranto* (1764), *gothic* was synonymous with supernatural horror; but, almost immediately, in the works of Ann Radcliffe and Clara M. Reeve, among others, the gothic took on a more sentimental and romantic character, almost as though the novels of Samuel Richardson had been overlaid with gothic props. Unlike the gothics of Walpole and Matthew Gregory Lewis, those of Radcliffe and Reeve used the supernatural for terror but demystified it by providing a logical explanation in the end. Radcliffe and Reeve both used the medieval period with its exotic trappings of chivalry to provide excitement. This latter type of gothic was the most influential and appealing in America in the early nineteenth century. After that, the word *gothic* was not again consistently applied to formula novels until recently, even though the form flourished in those years. In the early 1960s, Gerald Gross, an editor at Ace Books, used the term *gothic* to label a new paperback series of romantic mysteries designed for women readers. The term caught on immediately, and is now applied to a wide range of novels; gothics have been one of the most active and lucrative areas of publishing. However, the current gothic boom is hardly dependent upon new titles; many of the most popular books were published long ago, and either were never out of print or were returned to print to satisfy readers. The women's gothic novel was never truly out of vogue; it was merely submerged.

The term *romantic* is no less problematic since, in the literary sense, all popular fiction is romantic. Popular fiction is, in John Cawelti's phrase, a "moral fantasy" that allows its readers, who include a large number of literate Americans, to transcend the bounds of real life and enter a world in which things occur as they are "supposed to," where certain kinds of desired experiences can be lived vicariously.[2] Popular fiction is not realistic, is not intended to be by its authors, and is not desired to be by its readers. But because the term *romantic*, as used by Richard Chase and others to define a type of novel, applies to virtually all types of popular fiction, it is confusing to designate one particular formula as *romantic* in the narrower sense of that word.[3]

Another complication in the study of gothic and romantic fiction is the special literary relationship between the United States and Britain. From Ann Radcliffe's works to the Harlequin Romances, many of the most popular and influential gothic and romantic novels have been British imports; many of the American works are derivative. Both gothic and romantic fiction were "invented" in Britain, and British versions have been widely available in this country. Before the international copyright laws of the late nineteenth century, it was simple and cheap for American printers to pirate the works of British popular authors and pay no royalties. Benjamin Franklin, for example, reprinted Samuel Richardson's *Pamela* (1740-41) in Philadelphia as early as 1744. The audience for such fiction in recent years has been so insatiable that publishers have been obliged to reprint British authors to keep up with demand. Since 1960, for example, British novels dating back to the 1920s have been reprinted in American paperbacks. It seems arbitrary to limit consideration to American gothic and romantic fiction, since the reading public for these books seems not to discriminate between American and British authors. In addition, the derivative nature of some of the American examples makes discussion of British prototypes essential. One can hardly analyze *Charlotte Temple*, for example, without reference to *Pamela* and *Clarissa Harlowe*. Phyllis Whitney's works can be fruitfully compared to Charlotte Brontë's *Jane Eyre* (1847), Daphne du Maurier's *Rebecca* (1938), and the modern gothics of Victoria Holt. In a more tangential but still significant way, the work of Jane Austen elucidates the world of the Harlequin Romances. In any event, considerations of women's romances that take up the issue of the audience, rather than the authors and their works, cannot ignore the British primacy in both formulas.

Most scholars of popular culture would agree that analysis of popular culture materials tells us something about the audience; there is much less agreement on how to make the connection or what we can and cannot learn through the evaluation of fiction. Escape fiction certainly tells us some things about culture; we know, for example, that there are fads and styles in fiction in certain eras just as there are in fashion or music. We know that certain kinds of fiction go out of style; the pure seduction story died out after the first quarter of the nineteenth century and the erotic gothic was virtually unknown before the early 1970s. This crude comparison tells us something about sexual mores in the two periods, and it suggests something about women's values and norms. What it cannot do is provide information about women's behavior and about the delicate relationship between values and action. Because fiction is less a mirror of culture than a distorted window upon it, the use of fiction as cultural evidence is fraught with pitfalls and problems. Scholars who approach the evaluation of popular fiction from different academic disciplines differ in both their approaches and their conclusions; truly interdisciplinary studies have yet to emerge. There is no question that this mass of material, once reclaimed by researchers, will give us insight on women in America; certainly there is valid cultural information in a popular form that has persisted as long as gothic and romantic fiction. It is through rigorous investigation of the fiction itself, its publishing history, and its audience (insofar as that information is available), as well as the consideration of various interdisciplinary approaches to the analysis of this information, that we can understand its cultural significance. This book lays a foundation for that inquiry.

NOTES

1. Dashiell Hammett, *The Maltese Falcon*, in *The Novels of Dashiell Hammett* (New York: Alfred A. Knopf, 1966), p. 438.

2. John G. Cawelti, *Adventure, Mystery, and Romance: Formula Stories As Art and Popular Culture* (Chicago: University of Chicago Press, 1976), pp. 38-39.

3. Richard Chase, *The American Novel and Its Tradition* (Garden City, N.Y.: Doubleday, Anchor, 1957), pp. 12-20.

women's
gothic
and
romantic
fiction

CHAPTER I

History of Women's Gothic and Romantic Fiction

The roots of gothic and romantic fiction for women go back to the beginning of the novel itself as a literary form. If the putative origin of fiction, especially of published fiction for a relatively literate although otherwise heterogeneous audience, is Samuel Richardson's *Pamela* (1740-41), then the vital outlines of gothic and romantic fiction were established very early. The tensions of women's romances, the way the fictional world operates, were very much a part of *Pamela* and its host of imitations. Pamela was a serving girl in the household of a gentleman who tried every way he could imagine to seduce her. Written in a series of letters, the novel chronicles Pamela's resistance to him and his eventual capitulation in the face of her demonstrated virtue. Although *Pamela* is much longer than most women's romances, the central plot device of vicissitudes and trials giving way to a happy marriage is standard for such books. The reverse of this pattern developed very quickly thereafter in Richardson's *Clarissa Harlowe* (1747-48), in which the protagonist succumbs to her seducer and dies. Novels subsequent to these two repeated and elaborated these patterns, culminating in America in a series of novels of seduction that are among the earliest examples of prose fiction in this country's literary history. They also provide the first instance of America's continuing dependence upon British models for derivation of fictional patterns.

The first English gothic novels were also imported from England and widely read in America, where they became both popular and influential among the reading public and potential authors. The first of these was Horace Walpole's *The Castle of Otranto* (1764); he was followed by other British writers, including Ann Radcliffe, Clara M. Reeve, and Matthew Gregory "Monk" Lewis. The rise of the novel in America coincided with the peak of popularity for the gothic novel in England. Scholars and critics of gothic novels have divided the genre into categories; the most common distinctions are between the terror-gothic, the sentimental-gothic, and the historical-gothic. Terror-gothic novels, such as those of Walpole and Lewis, emphasize the supernatural, sometimes using depraved monks and nuns as villains. The influence of this gothic form was most marked upon serious novelists in America, who used the supernatural to explore psychological states and the meaning of evil. It was the sentimental-gothic, however, that most influenced popular novelists in this country and was most popular among readers. The primary writer of this kind of gothic was Radcliffe, who used the supernatural for suspense but always revealed a human hand behind her effects. The historical-gothic also influenced American writers because of its way of romanticizing the past, usually with anachronistic elements, using the strangeness of earlier times to augment the atmosphere of terror. The popular audience in America was attracted to sensation, but preferred to have the supernatural eventually explained.

Fiction in general was a suspect and controversial form of literature on both sides of the Atlantic during the eighteenth and early nineteenth centuries. Suspected of wielding a malevolent influence over their readers, particularly young and impressionable girls, many writers found it necessary to construct elaborate defenses of their work; many claimed their novels were based on fact. Even Samuel Richardson found it prudent to defend *Pamela* against critics who charged it with prurience. But the attacks on fiction continued, perhaps most ironically and skillfully in Jane Austen's *Northanger Abbey* (1818), in which she portrays a young woman whose head has been turned by her extensive reading of gothic novels to the point where she looks for adventure in even the most mundane situations. Other circumstances retarded the development of a full novelistic tradition in America. American critics often attacked fiction simply because it was "untrue." In addition, the traditional elements of the setting of British fiction, such as ancient castles, sinister monasteries, and a hierarchical social order, were notably absent in America. International copyright laws were not established until the late nineteenth century, putting American writers at a distinct disadvantage until then, since American printers could so easily and inexpensively reprint British books without paying royalties to their authors. American authors in this early period of fiction faced a paucity of literary tradition, a disadvantageous economic structure in publishing, and a group of articulate, influential, and often hostile critics.

The first "American" example of a romantic novel was probably Susanna Haswell Rowson's *Charlotte Temple* (1791), one of the great bestsellers in American literary history. First published in Britain by a woman who emigrated to America to set up a school for young ladies, *Charlotte Temple* went through more than two hundred printings, forty of them before Susanna Rowson's death in 1824. The first American edition was published in Philadelphia in 1794. As late as the early part of the twentieth century, the book was still in print in the United States, one 1905 edition complete with photographs, including one of Charlotte's reputed grave in New York City. *Charlotte Temple* was a classic seduction story in which the young and innocent protagonist allows herself to be carried off to America by a military officer; when she becomes pregnant, he abandons her, leaving her to die miserably after giving birth to a daughter, whose life was later chronicled by Rowson in *Lucy Temple; or, Charlotte's Daughter* (1828). Several later books by authors claimed to prove that Charlotte's story was true, indicating an intense interest in this book; women made pilgrimages to Charlotte's grave throughout the nineteenth century.

Many other seduction novels were published in the early nineteenth century. Hannah W. Foster's *The Coquette* (1797), Eliza Vicery's *Emily Hamilton* (1803), and several anonymous novels such as *Fidelity Rewarded* (1796) and *Amelia; or, The Faithless Briton* (1798), told versions of the familiar tale. Most of these, incidentally, were presented to the public as true stories, thinly disguised by changing names and places. Since seduction stories served so consciously as cautionary tales, the claim for their truth is logical, although it might be just as reasonable to conclude that the novelists claimed a basis in fact to combat the prejudice against fiction. But after the early nineteenth century, the full-blown novel of seduction was hard to find. The tensions of the precarious position in which a "loose woman" could find herself were still important in later romantic novels, but the explicit warning about men, the specific if somewhat euphemistic story about the dangers of sexuality, was less significant in romantic fiction.

Charles Brockden Brown was the first American author to use the gothic in his fiction; moreover, he was much more skillful than most of his contemporaries. His novels, including *Wieland* (1798), *Ormond* (1799), and *Edgar Huntly* (1799), use American settings but they differ significantly from women's gothic because the love story does not have an equal place in the story. Brown did provide rational explanations for his apparently supernatural effects, although he used the gothic more to explore psychological states and experiments than to exploit the sensational possibilities of the material. A lesser contemporary of Brown was Isaac Mitchell, the author of one of the most popular novels of the period, *The Asylum; or, Alonzo and Melissa* (1804), a gothic romance hinging upon the opposition of a father to his daughter's proposed marriage. Mitchell went so far as to place a medieval castle on Long Island from which Alonzo rescues Melissa after a series of gothic adventures. On the other hand, Sally Wood's *Julia; or, The Illuminated Baron* (1800), another novel that is close to British models, is set in eighteenth-century France. The book's plot depends upon the hidden identities of Julia and her suitor, who endure many dangers before being united. In the end, both are revealed to be aristocrats, but they renounce their titles, out of the author's deference to American democratic sentiment. Many traditional gothic elements are present, including a dangerous chateau, visits to tombs, kidnappings, and an attempted rape. Other novels by Wood include *Dorval; or, The Speculator* (1801), *Amelia; or, The Influence of Virtue: An Old Man's Story* (1802?), and *Ferdinand and Elmira: A Russian Story* (1804). Wood was from Maine.

Other important early novels include *Monima; or, The Beggar Girl* (1802) by Martha Read, *Adelaide* (1816) by Margaret Botsford, the anonymous *Female American* (1800?), and *The Step-Mother* (1799) by Helena Wells. *Laura* (1809) by "A Lady of Philadelphia" is about a nun who comes to America and endures many terrors in a yellow-fever epidemic. Ann Eliza Bleecker and the anonymous "Lady of Massachusetts" also wrote fiction in this period. The relative significance of American books to the reading public in America at this time seems to have been slight. In *The Sentimental Novel in America*, Herbert Ross Brown analyzes the catalogue of Caritat's, a popular circulating library in New York. He notes that only 18 of 1171 titles of fiction in the 1799 edition were by American authors. The list, however, included many examples of gothic and romantic fiction: 331 novels were by women; 143 were described as epistolary; 45 were gothic; 135, didactic; 98, sentimental; and 23, Oriental, all possible categories in which gothic and romantic fiction might be found.[1] In addition to hardcover fiction, gothic and romantic stories were also sometimes found in more ephemeral media such as magazines and chapbooks.

After the heyday of the gothic novel in Britain and America around the turn of the century, the tradition splintered in a number of different directions. Poe was influenced by gothic conventions in his stories of horror as well as in his stories of detection. Science fiction was also indebted to gothic fiction for its premise of the seemingly supernatural or strange explained by rational means. The melodrama often resembled gothic fiction in world view as well as in conventions. Some critics have even suggested that the Western was influenced by the gothic, especially in its use of the wilderness and Indians as sources of danger. However, all of these uses of the gothic go beyond the original gothic forms and also far beyond the imaginative world posited by female gothic novelists.

Because the American democratic and practical mind was never quite comfortable with the gothic novel of terror, except for a few notably sensational examples such as George Lippard's *The Quaker City; or, The Monks of Monk's Hall* (1844) or Maria Monk's *Awful Disclosures* (1836), the true heirs of the gothic novel are some of the more adventurous of the women's novels of the nineteenth and twentieth centuries, others of which would be characterized more accurately as romantic. Many writers of sentimental romances also wrote novels that today would be published as gothics, novels that are dependent upon the models of Radcliffe and the Brontës, among others, for their plots and their world view. Even at their most tame, the domestic and sentimental novelists often relied upon gothic conventions for suspense. The more romantic examples of the type build upon the conventions set down by Richardson and Jane Austen, among others. By the 1840s, the gothic-romantic continuum in women's fiction was well established in its current form.

From the 1820s until after the Civil War, gothic and romantic fiction for women was dominated by a group of novelists usually referred to as the domestic sentimentalists, even though some of them wrote very exciting books that were less domestic than adventurous. The work of this group of women has been more thoroughly analyzed and documented than in any other period of women's fiction. Although critics disagree, sometimes diametrically, over the meaning of these novels, there seems little doubt that these books, at their most fundamental, tell stories about relationships between men and women, differing mostly in the circumstances of the characters; those in gothics have adventures and are threatened by outside dangers, while those in the more romantic novels must learn to be domestic, virtuous women in order to achieve their goals. Some writers wrote novels of both kinds.

Among the most popular writers of the antebellum period were Catharine Maria Sedgwick, Lydia Maria Child, Fanny Fern (pseudonym of Ruth Payton Willis), Mary Jane Holmes, Ann Sophia Stephens, Maria Susanna Cummins, Harriet Foster Cheney, Caroline Chesebro', Eliza Foster Cushing, Caroline Lee Hentz, Fanny Forrester (pseudonym of

Emily Judson), Maria Jane McIntosh, Elizabeth Oakes Smith, and Susan and Anna Warner. These women spanned a whole range of types of fiction, but most of them wrote at least one book in the gothic or romantic mode. Many of their books were domestic romances, showing a woman, often bereft of male support, solving domestic difficulties, improving her character, saving souls, learning to be a "true woman"; but despite the trials of domestic life, the reconciliation with woman's place in a good marriage is where the plot ends. These were the novels that prompted Nathaniel Hawthorne's heartfelt cry in a letter to his publisher in 1855, a few years after *The Scarlet Letter* (1850) had been less than enthusiastically received by the mass reading audience.

America is now wholly given over to a d——d mob of scribbling women, and I should have no chance of success while the public taste is occupied with their trash—and should be ashamed of myself if I did succeed. What is the mystery of these innumerable editions of the "Lamplighter," and other books neither better nor worse?—worse they could not be, and better they need not be, when they sell by the 100,000.[2]

It is ironic to note that the output of women's romantic novels included a rather large number of historical fictions about women in Puritan New England, some of whom ran afoul of the religious and civil authorities of the colony, although for offenses more acceptable to nineteenth-century taste than was adultery. Hawthorne might be forgiven if he found contemptible the audience that embraced Catharine Maria Sedgwick's *Hope Leslie* (1827) and Eliza B. Lee's *Naomi* (1848) more willingly than it did his novel of Hester Prynne.

Some of those novels of Puritan New England had gothic elements, as well as romantic ones. Pairs of lovers were kept apart by parents, or by social and religious differences; the problems were complicated by the hostile environment of the New World, often including adventures in Indian camps or in the wilderness. More important, perhaps, was a continuing plot element in many of these books in which the young heroines exhibited a degree of liberality and religious toleration that was comfortable for nineteenth-century readers but would have been anathema to Puritan authorities. Over and over, these characters assert the worth of the individual and of conscience against the repressive and retrogressive New England leaders.[3] Especially significant in the group of Puritan novels are *Hobomok: A Tale of Early Times* (1824) by Lydia Maria Child, *A Peep at the Pilgrims in Sixteen Hundred Thirty-Six* (1824) by Harriet Vaughn Cheney, *Hope Leslie* (1827) by Catharine Maria Sedgwick, and the anonymous *The Witch of New England: A*

Romance (1824). There were at least thirty such novels before *The Scarlet Letter*.

Among the domestic sentimentalists, the work of Catharine Maria Sedgwick probably ranks highest. Sedgwick in her own time was favorably compared to James Fenimore Cooper, although her reputation has proved less durable than his (most of her books are out of print). In a series of novels, she described young women caught in difficult situations who prove their characters through a series of trials. These women are no shrinking violets like the heroines of the earlier seduction novels; they make decisions on the basis of conscience and morality and they are active in the plots. Sedgwick and her contemporaries were less simplistic in their valuing of marriage for women than the earlier novelists were, but their heroines all marry in the end (including that of Sedgwick's late novel *Married or Single?* [1857], in which she explores the issue of the necessity of marriage for all women). Sedgwick's novels are sometimes adventurous, set in historical periods, with elements that some critics defined as gothic. She also, however, seems to have been consciously writing against the sentimental tradition by attempting to construct models of behavior for women who marry only after their character is formed and who can be valued by the men around them for their qualities of integrity and maturity. Her portrayals of marriage include both practical and romantic elements.

Other authors followed Sedgwick's lead in portraying heroines whose possession of "womanly" qualities gave them the proper attributes for mature marriages. In one of the biggest sellers of the nineteenth century, Augusta Jane Evans Wilson's *St. Elmo* (1867), the heroine, Edna Earl, is a woman who would prefer to support herself rather than accept a less-than-satisfactory marriage. She refuses to play the woman's role of redeemer for her dissolute lover, demanding instead that he straighten out his own life without her help. When he does, she can marry him in full confidence of his worthiness for her. But despite the prevalence of strong heroines in these novels, the exaltation of "feminine" virtues and the eventual marriage always forms the core of the plot. Absence of weakness and dependence does not provide a substitute for marriage, and in almost every domestic novel of the period, the woman, no matter what the details of the individual plot, ends up in a happy marriage. There is probably an element of "having it both ways" in these books, since they counsel women to cultivate the aspects of their characters that suit them especially well to be good wives and mothers. In the view of many of these authors, those qualities did not lead women to be doormats or to repress their active sides in order to win economic security at all costs. In a reversal of our stereotypes of Victorian women, those qualities are seen instead as absolutely essential to mature relationships. The ambivalence is clear, however, in the number of women who manage, one way or another, to scrape through their difficulties, to demonstrate their ability to exist autonomously with a measure of integrity and respect, only to win lasting joy through marriage. Some critics might argue that this pattern reflects a failure of the imagination: the nineteenth century offered very few acceptable and remunerative roles for women outside of marriage, thus the authors were unable to end their books satisfactorily in any other way without suggesting a continuation of the hard times and difficulties of the plots.

By the mid-nineteenth century, the novels of women authors were well established in the literary market place. Particularly prolific and popular was E. D. E. N. Southworth, whose literary career spans almost half the century. In books like *The Hidden Hand* (1859) and *The Curse of Clifton* (1852), she used many gothic conventions such as lost heirs, evil villains, virtuous maidens, nobles, and castles in exotic settings, in novels that accurately reflect the world view of gothic fiction. That world, by the mid-nineteenth century, could be defined as one in which life itself was precarious, and especially so for young women. The romantic happiness of a young girl was always vulnerable to the machinations of villains or to minor moral peccadillos of her own. Southworth's novels were published in a variety of ways, in newspapers, in periodicals, and in series of dime novels; and many of her books were issued more than once, on occasion with new titles. They were very long, written in a highly romantic style, and full of coincidence in plot and anachronism in setting. They were usually written very quickly, in order to satisfy the voracious appetite of their large audience and to keep Southworth solvent.

Another important phenomenon of the period was "Bertha M. Clay," the pseudonym for a group of writers, beginning with Charlotte M. Breame, who wrote women's novels in the gothic mode for Street and Smith's dime novel series. The popularity of the pure gothic in this period is further demonstrated by the fact that one of the major publishers of dime novels, Norman Munro, once published Horace Walpole's *The Castle of Otranto* (1764) in a story paper without acknowledging the source by either author or title.

Although the work of the domestic sentimentalists before the war was still in print and often very popular in the postwar period, much of the gothic and romantic fiction of the time seems to have been in less permanent form than the traditional novel. Series of dime novels from a variety of publishers included gothic and romantic titles among their better-known Western and detective stories. Weekly story papers also thrived on the form. Because of the ephemeral nature of this serialized material, less is known about the authors and scope of the fiction, but hardback versions were sometimes published even if the work had been serialized in periodicals earlier. Romantic novels about working girls, written by Laura Jean Libbey, were especially popular; and toward the end of the period, historical fiction, much of which falls into gothic or romantic modes, had a widespread vogue.

Historical periods that had formerly not seemed appropriate to fiction were becoming more prevalent in the work of popular authors. In the early nineteenth century, gothic novels relied almost entirely upon the medieval period for background, and in both gothic and romantic fiction (if a historical setting was used) periods no more recent than two centuries before were most common. The novelists of the antebellum period, however, found material in the colonial era of America and, also, to a lesser degree, in the Revolutionary War period. By the late nineteenth century, novels about the Revolution were common, and authors increasingly found the American past a much more fruitful source for fiction than had earlier authors. Distance in time, of course, is probably the main reason for the shift. After the Centennial celebration of 1876, the heroic and romantic aspects of the American past were certified as significant and truly historical. Popular conceptions of conditions in earlier times were based more upon imaginative re-creation of the past than upon memory or professional historical literature. This trend was extended by the twentieth century's discovery of the Victorian and turn-of-the-century periods for modern gothic fiction.

As each era's literature finds material in later and later historical periods, writers impose upon the past the concerns and conventions about the status of women and definitions of value that are relevant to their own audience. The limitations of women's lives and the importance of male-female relationships can be dramatized through the device of placing these events in a past era less enlightened than that of the author. The most prominent of the historical novelists of the late nineteenth and early twentieth centuries was Mary Johnston, a native Virginian. Johnston frequently used Virginia history in her novels; the most popular and enduring of these was *To Have and To Hold* (1900), which has been in print during most of the intervening years since its publication. A straightforward melodrama set in colonial Virginia, the novel focuses upon the plight of a young woman who comes to Virginia in a shipment of brides. The precarious lives of women in the past are well illustrated by this plot device, for these characters are totally dependent upon the good nature and goodwill of the men who choose them. Johnston's use of this device depends more upon the reaction of her contemporary audience than upon any concrete information about how such brides may have felt at the time. The novel shows women claimed, married, and taken the same day to the home that would be theirs for the rest of their lives. Into this situation she thrusts her heroine, who had been a ward of the king while in England. She is selected by Ralph Percy, a young farmer with an aristocratic name, who treats her with great respect, not forcing her into the intimacies of marriage until they know each other and fall in love. His protection is important for her because she is fleeing the attentions of a villain who had tried to seduce her in England. He follows her to America and the dangers in the plot arise from his pursuit and from the depradations of the Indians who attack the colony.

Other romantic writers of this period included Amelia E. Barr and Isabella Alden. Barr was born in England, moved to America, and wrote more than sixty novels, including a series of historical novels about the development of Manhattan. Her books have been much less durable than those of Johnston. Alden, known as "Pansy," wrote romantic novels as well as advice books, popular history, and Bible studies; she also edited a children's magazine. She influenced her niece Grace Livingston Hill, who was to be a very popular romantic author of the twentieth century. Hill's work is mostly domestic melodrama, although she combined her romantic plots with sections of prose that read like evangelical Protestant tracts. Much of her work is still available in paperback and seems to have an enduring audience, although one suspects it is made up of older readers.

Lists of bestsellers dated after 1895 are readily available, so the task of identifying trends and authors in fiction becomes easier, although the problem of finding material that did not reach the bestseller lists remains. The lists, however, do show that love stories and gothics were in vogue and that there had been relatively little change in the basic value patterns of the fiction. Mystery stories by women writers often had romantic and gothic overtones. Mary Roberts Rinehart and Mignon Eberhart, for example, both better known for their detective stories, also wrote gothic and romantic novels. Rinehart and Eberhart specialized in detective stories about middle-aged spinsters, who solved mysteries much as male detectives did. These older women, like Agatha Christie's Miss Marple, were beyond the age of romance. However, in many other novels, both Rinehart and Eberhart featured young, romantic women who married at the end. Rinehart also wrote straightforward, non-mysterious romances. Another very popular author of domestic romantic novels was Kathleen Norris, whose work appears on bestseller lists through the period.

One of the great success stories in the twentieth century among writers of women's gothic and romantic fiction is that of Emilie Loring, whose work began appearing in the 1920s. Loring, a Boston matron, was born in the 1860s (date uncertain) and died in 1951. Her books appeared with regularity through the 1930s and 1940s and were set in the present. All were highly romantic, often including plot elements of international or industrial espionage. Her books have been in print in paperback for some time, but there is a mystery about her later work that has not been satisfactorily resolved. Loring died in 1951, but her publisher continued to issue books under her name into the 1970s. There is no evidence as to whether she actually wrote them or not, but one suspects that another author or authors, unknown to date, took over both her formula and her name. Biographical information on Loring is difficult to obtain. Fannie Hurst and Faith Baldwin also obtained significant success in the romantic genre during this period.

The 1930s saw the publication of two highly significant romantic novels, *Gone With the Wind* (1936) and, in England, Daphne du Maurier's *Rebecca* (1938), which was to become the modern prototype for the gothic romance. Both of these books were so exceptionally popular among a wide audience that for some time their intimate relationship to and dependence upon earlier models of gothic and romantic fiction were overlooked. As suggested previously, *Gone With the Wind* exemplifies the "antiromance," in which the protagonist behaves in such a manner as to lose her true love. Scarlett's egocentricity, her willingness to express her forbidden love for Ashley Wilkes, her lack of "normal" feminine loyalty, her inability to recognize how much she loves Rhett until the very end, her willful refusal to act as a good wife should in any of her three marriages, all amply demonstrate, to an audience conditioned to respond to those cues, why she fails at love. In case Scarlett's own behavior is not enough to convince an audience of the rightness of the ending, *Gone With the Wind* also has Melanie as a major character. She is everything Scarlett is not, although she lacks Scarlett's strength, resolution, and ability. Melanie is loyal to others, even when she has reason to distrust them; she always thinks the best of people she cares for; she is nurturing, even toward Scarlett's husbands; she clearly earns her marital happiness with Ashley. The genius of *Gone With the Wind* as a romantic novel is that Margaret Mitchell managed to create two women, both of whom the reader cares about, who are such diametrical opposites. The story, told with Melanie at the center, could not have attracted the audience that the book did, because Melanie's "feminine" but bland reactions and actions could hardly have enhanced the drama of the historical period. However, given the value structure of the book, Scarlett's triumphs in the outside world, holding her family together, keeping Tara, getting food into the mouths of her dependents, almost incapacitate her for normal domestic life.

In the case of *Rebecca*, Daphne du Maurier wrote a more conventional book in the genre of gothic romance, but did it so skillfully that authors are still copying her. Her protagonist is nameless, an orphan working as a companion to a rich, obnoxious woman who exploits her, destroys her confidence, and embarrasses her with rude behavior. At a vacation spot, the girl meets the mysterious Maximilian de Winter, whose beautiful wife Rebecca has died. Maximilian, assumed by all to be in deep mourning, unaccountably proposes to the heroine, who is far too modest and naive to think he is doing anything other than a favor to a girl for whom he feels sorry. They return to Manderley, his Cornish mansion, where she is haunted by the memories of Rebecca. Rebecca's things are still in the house in their old places; Rebecca's servants and friends make both overt and covert comparisons, always invidious, between the two wives; the house is still run exactly as Rebecca wished, and the girl is ignorant of protocol in such matters. She retreats further and further into her imagination, assuming that Max has changed nothing because, in his grief, he cannot bear to speak or think about Rebecca. Gradually, the story comes out. Rebecca had been both cruel and vain, an unfaithful wife, and a wicked, manipulative woman. Finding she had cancer, she provoked Max into killing her, thinking he would be caught and she could triumph over him posthumously. But he was not caught. The secret haunts him and he cannot bear to think about Rebecca because of his guilt. The heroine manages to help him avoid arrest, but Manderley burns, and they leave Cornwall. She tells her own story years later while she is serving as Max's nurse, a position reminiscent of that of Jane Eyre at the end of Charlotte Brontë's novel.

These two books were made into extremely popular motion pictures, and some forty years later both the books and the movies are readily available to modern audiences. They seem to have lost none of their popularity. There is no question, also, that both of these books (and both of these films) appeal to a male as well as to a female audience. In the late 1930s and early 1940s, a number of gothic or romantic films were made in Hollywood. This seems, however, to be the peak period for such films, since Hollywood is understandably reluctant to make many films that primarily appeal to a female audience. *Gone With the Wind*, *Forever Amber*, *Pride and Prejudice*, and *Jane Eyre* were all produced during this period; and some directors, most notably Alfred Hitchcock, produced a few other films of the type using original or less well known material. Both Joan Fontaine and Ingrid Bergman were particularly successful in this kind of film.

The post-World War II period has been a very fruitful one for popular gothic and romantic fiction in America, and this is the period since the early nineteenth century when it is most difficult to limit discussion to American authors as opposed to British writers. In 1960, the first novel by Victoria Holt (pseudonym of Eleanor Burford Hibbert) was published in America. Its author had written romantic novels since 1945 under a variety of pseudonyms (Kathleen Kellow, Elbur Ford, and Jean Plaidy). *Mistress of Mellyn* started the gothic vogue of recent years, during which publishers in America have been in great competition for material. The book's significance is that it seems to have whetted readers' interest once again for gothic fiction, although without offering anything especially new. One reviewer, in fact, noted that it is a not-so-subtle reworking of *Rebecca*. The main character, Martha Leigh, takes a job as a governess at the home of Connan TreMellyn, a wealthy Cornish landowner whose child is a "problem." Martha learns how to handle the child, bringing her out of her shell. She also learns that Alvean is not Connan's child, and that his beautiful wife ran away with her lover, leaving him with the child. Martha later discovers, however, that Connan was not grieving for his unfaithful wife and that, in fact, the wife had been murdered by a rival and had not run away at all. Connan loves Martha, although, like the nameless woman in *Rebecca*, she is so used to thinking of herself as negligible that she cannot believe it. By the end of the story, she has shown Connan his responsibility toward Alvean, restored his faith in women, and has also, braving the danger involved, discovered the identity of the first wife's killer.

During the early 1960s, after the publication of *Mistress of Mellyn*, American publishers began their own series of gothic novels, in hardback and paperback, relying upon British and American reprints and originals. Some publishers began reprinting the work of popular British gothic and romantic writers such as Georgette Heyer, Barbara Cartland, and Dorothy Eden, occasionally reprinting books from as early as the 1920s. Mary Stewart, another popular British writer, also benefited from the American taste for such fiction. She had earned some American attention in the late 1950s—her *Nine Coaches Waiting* (1958) was serialized in *Ladies' Home Journal*—but her real popularity occurred in the wake of *Mistress of Mellyn*. American authors also saw an increased interest in their fiction. Phyllis Whitney had been writing romantic mysteries for women before Holt's success; by the late 1960s she found herself the premier American writer of such work. She still publishes one book per year in the gothic mode. Anya Seton has published fewer works, although one of her earliest, *Dragonwyck* (1944), was a pure gothic novel set in a mansion on the Hudson River. Most of her books are historical romances with gothic overtones. Other important authors who emerged subsequent to 1960 were Susan Howatch, Daoma Winston, Dorothy Daniels (pseudonym of Norman Daniels), Catherine Gaskin, and Evelyn Anthony. At the present time, there are hundreds of imitators of the major writers, many of whom publish only in paperback originals.

The books today fall into several related categories. Some are gothic novels with contemporary settings in which the strange events derive from the exotic nature of the setting; an example is Phyllis Whitney's *Black Amber* (1964), set in Turkey. Others are classic gothic stories in which a young woman (governess, new bride) endures the terrors of an old house with ancient legends, superstitions, and family secrets; an example is Phyllis Whitney's *Domino* (1979). Many of these are set in the past. Others are novels about historical or pseudohistorical women, their stories told in gothic or romantic terms; two of the most popular of these have been Anya Seton's *Katherine* (1954) and *Devil Water* (1962). Others are Regency Romances, frothy romantic tales about the Regency period in England, written by Georgette Heyer, Barbara Cartland, Clare Darcy, and others.

In the 1970s, there were two significant new trends in gothic and romantic fiction, although they did not diminish the popularity of the other types. The new erotic gothics, by such authors as Rosemary Rogers, Kathleen Woodiwiss, Claire Lorimer, and Lolah Burford, have all been originally published in paperback, but they are much longer than most of the other novels. Rogers's *Wicked, Loving Lies* (1976) is set in eighteenth- and nineteenth-century Spain, England, France, Tripoli, Louisiana, and Texas. The heroine is raped innumerable times, usually by the same man in different guises (he is, of course, the hero). She is, for a time, Napoleon's mistress, a prisoner in a harem, a British noblewoman, a quadroon slave in the South, and an heiress. Lolah Burford's *Alyx* (1977) is about a woman and a man who are white slaves on a breeding plantation in the Caribbean. They are put together nightly in a breeding hut to produce a slave child. Although they never see each other in daylight, they fall in love and conspire to escape.

The second important trend, although almost the antithesis of the first, is the growing popularity in America of the pure light romance, so long popular among the British reading public. Represented best by the Harlequin Romances, a Canadian subsidiary of the British firm of Mills and Boon, these books are often sold in large quantities. Harlequin, for example, has subscribers who receive, for about $7.60 per month, eight new Harlequin novels and a magazine. Reported sales for Harlequin for 1979 were 158 million copies. There are other series of Harlequins available as well, including historical romances and Mystiques (gothics). Simon and Schuster, which distributed Harlequins in the United States until late 1979, has established its own series of paperback romances. Other publishers followed suit in 1979 and early 1980. These books are pure romance; sex is handled with great discretion and the double standard is endemic. The striking contrasts between the two newer forms for the gothic and romantic market merely highlight the insatiability of the audience and its growing heterogeneity.

Magazines have also flourished on love stories and light mysteries in their fiction pages, from the most serious and uplifting of the women's magazines, such as *Godey's Ladies Book* and *Good Housekeeping*, to the confession magazines, love comics, and pulps, the twentieth-century versions of nineteenth-century story papers.

Despite superficial changes over the two centuries of their popularity, the formulas for the various types of gothic and romantic fiction appear to be remakably stable. Seduction stories have given way to erotic gothics; medieval settings, to Victorian; domestic trivia, to world travel. But the outlines of the fictional world are, in the larger sense, much more firm than they may seem. The stories still occur in a world in which marriage is seen as the best of all possible states for women and in a world that, because women have very little control over their lives, is especially precarious for them. Despite the irrationality of such dangers in a twentieth-century context, gothic novels are still full of old houses, corrupt aristocrats, supernatural effects rationally explained, and melodramatic reconciliations. The value system for women in modern romantic fiction is also very similar to that of earlier models. The necessity for virtuous behavior and the punishment for transgression, except in erotic gothics, as well as the very definition of femininity, are relative constants in such fiction.

What this suggests is that since the beginning of romantic fiction for women, in all its various forms, women have been interested in and satisfied by reading experiences that are substantially unchanged. In the absence of good critical studies and bibliographies, it is difficult to say just how widespread gothic and romantic fiction for women has been in American literary history. But the evidence is clear enough to indicate that it has been both pervasive and persistent and that subsequent research will reveal a great quantity of such fiction that did not reach the bestseller lists or succeed as individual novels but that has had a remarkably stable form and devoted audience over time.

NOTES

1. Herbert Ross Brown, *The Sentimental Novel in America* (Durham, N.C.: Duke University Press, 1940).

2. Nathaniel Hawthorne, quoted in ibid., p. 179.

3. See Michael Davitt Bell, *Hawthorne and the Historical Romance of New England* (Princeton, N.J.: Princeton University Press, 1971).

CHAPTER 2

Bibliographies, Reference Works, and Sources for the Study of Major Authors of Gothic and Romantic Fiction

Because there is so little agreement about the definitions and categories relating to both gothic and romantic fiction, and because, until recently, there has been so little critical interest in these forms, there are no specialized bibliographies or reference tools to identify titles, authors, or critical essays in a consistent way. There are, however, standard and specialized bibliographies and reference works that include such books, even if they index them in different ways. Searching for gothic and romantic fiction in such volumes is not an easy task, but if a few key indicators are kept in mind, it can be a rewarding one. Bibliographies of fiction, for example, can be used by looking for female authors and considering the implications of the titles: do they sound romantic? do they sound adventurous? Of course, there is then no substitute for actually locating the novel and reading sections of it to ascertain the outlines of the plot, the characteristics of the hero and heroine, and the point of view. Bibliographies with plot summaries are especially helpful. Other bibliographies, on specialized types of fiction, can be very good sources, as can histories or bibliographies relating to the publishing industry or to such topics as books in series. In the absence of bibliographical works that specifically treat such fiction, many of the sources that are useful can aid both in identifying titles, authors, and bibliographical material and in finding critical and analytical material that bears upon the formulas.

The problem of locating good sources is compounded because women authors have historically been taken less seriously and studied less frequently than men. This bias, coupled with the ephemeral nature of so much gothic and romantic fiction, means that there are few full-length studies of writers in this genre. On the other hand, some writers have been the subjects of dissertations, or of journal articles, by scholars looking for a subject outside the usual range of topics. This chapter surveys the best resources for locating titles and authors relevant to gothic and romantic fiction, standard reference guides that may be of some aid, studies of individual writers, and collections of papers and manuscripts relating to individual writers. Major research collections are described in Appendix 1.

When dealing with such a loosely defined topic, it is probably best to begin with the most basic kind of reference guide for fiction. For example, Gerald B. Cotton and Hilda Mary McGill's *Fiction Guides, General: British and American* is an essential tool, an excellent bibliographical guide with much American material, and especially valuable since the cataloguing of fiction in libraries is rarely refined beyond author and title. The book is described as a "comprehensive survey of guides to and other works dealing with fiction" and it should not be overlooked.

There are also many general guides to the study of literature, mostly research handbooks and often for beginners, that can be helpful. Listed in these are usually the most basic reference tools to literature in general; many of those tools, however, include popular material and some gothic and romantic fiction in their listings. Most notable of these is Robert C. Schweik and Dieter Riesner's *Reference Sources in English and American Literature: An Annotated Bibliography*. The volume is an excellent comprehensive guide to sources, is annotated, and includes useful hints for researchers. The American section is long and comprehensive and there are additional sections on interdisciplinary literary materials, microforms and reprints, media, dissertations, serials, reviews, biographical information, and pseudonyms. Clarence Gohdes's *Bibliographical Guide to the Study of the Literature of the United States of America* is a good annotated bibliography of journals, reference guides, critical works, and reprints. The annotations often quote from the works. *Guide to Basic Information Sources in English Literature* by Paul A. Doyle is fairly comprehensive and, despite the title, includes American information. F. W. Bateson and Harrison T. Messerole's *A Guide to English and American Literature* is a good narrative bibliography of sources but has little American material, although there is information on the novel in general. These sources, of course, lead only to other bibliographical tools, none of which is directly on the subject of gothic and romantic fiction, although many may be useful.

A more specific source is Patsy C. Howard's *Theses in American Literature, 1896-1971.* Academia being what it is, many scholars over the years have chosen to write on fairly obscure authors, sometimes those who wrote gothic or romantic fiction. For example, the Howard volume lists six theses on Caroline Lee Hentz and four on Mary Johnston. Other thesis and dissertation guides, such as James Woodress's *Dissertations in American Literature, 1891-1955, Supplement, 1956-1961* should also be consulted.

General fiction listings of various types can repay browsing, although some are much easier to use than others. Perhaps the major tool that now exists for finding gothic and romantic novels themselves, and for surveying an author's canon, is a massive three-set guide in twenty-five volumes entitled *Bibliography of English Language Fiction in the Library of Congress Through 1950*, compiled by R. Glenn Wright. These volumes are composed of reproduced cards from the Library of Congress shelflist. Each of the three sets has its own title: *Author Bibliography of English Language Fiction in the Library of Congress Through 1950, Chronological Bibliography of English Language Fiction in the Library of Congress Through 1950*, and *Title Bibliography of English Language Fiction in the Library of Congress Through 1950.* Because the cards themselves are reproduced, and the compiler went to some trouble to find biographical information that could be added to the cards before reproduction, there is much information that would not be available in a standard bibliographical format. The Library of Congress, as the nation's copyright depository, has many of the novels published in the United States over a long period of time. Of course, the collection is not complete—nothing could be—but researchers lucky enough to have access to it can find a wealth of fiction that in other institutions would either not have been purchased or not have been saved.

The Wright *Bibliography* is organized within each of the three sets by author's nationality, and there are additional indexes to translators and translations. Particularly for the early period, when not many novels were being published in America and the Library of Congress was little more than a library for the Congress, the chronological section of the bibliography is exceptionally useful. One can survey the entries through about 1825 or so in a short period of time, and much relevant material is listed. For the later period, the author bibliography is useful, because once an author has been identified as having written romantic or gothic fiction, an entire survey of the author's work in the Library of Congress is readily available. The chronological listings are useful for studies of particular time periods, such as the tracing of the influence of a particular bestseller on other authors who try to imitate its success. Although not all books written in English are represented, the Library of Congress collection is comprehensive enough to make this bibliography an excellent and useful source.

At the Library of Congress, fiction is catalogued in its own classes (PZ3, for authors whose first book was published prior to 1950, and PZ4, for those whose first book was after 1950). The Wright *Bibliography* covers the PZ3 category but omits PZ4. Many of the books listed are now housed in the Rare Book Room. Often, a book's location in that collection will be noted on the card, but occasionally it is not. There is a specialized card catalogue in the Rare Book Room. For the New York Public Library, another major depository of popular fiction, dictionary catalogues of many of the special collections are available in libraries around the country and can be especially helpful. The *Dictionary Catalog of the Rare Book Division*, the *Dictionary Catalog* of the Manuscript Division, and the *Dictionary Catalog of the Henry W. and Albert A. Berg Collection of English and American Literature* are all useful in determining data about gothic and romantic fiction and in ascertaining what is held by that library.

Lyle H. Wright has made a career of tracking down early American imprints in fiction and publishing annotated lists of such books, so all of his bibliographies should be used for finding titles. An early edition in 1939, *American Fiction, 1774-1850*, is a bibliography of American fiction in nineteen major collections as of that date. It has lists by authors (if known), locations of copies, numbers of pages, and sizes of books. There are some descriptive annotations. There is also an appendix of unexamined titles taken from various sources, along with a title index. Two later volumes updating the list are *American Fiction, 1774-1850* and *American Fiction, 1774-1900*. The second of these announces plans to put the selected volumes on microcard and microfiche. Another good source for early American imprints is Charles Evans's *American Bibliography*. Although it helps to know which titles or authors to look for, the *Author Catalog and Title Catalog* of the Microbook Library of American Civilization lists some novels, and all works in the Microbook Library are on ultrafiche. Entries on title refer back to full entries on authors.

A 1968 reprint of an 1891 guide to fiction, *Descriptive Lists of American International Romantic and British Novels*, compiled by William M. Griswold, is an odd but exceptionally good source for nineteenth-century works. The book is divided into sections: "Novels of American Country Life," "Novels of American City Life," "International Novels," "Romantic Novels," and "British Novels." It includes annotations on each book with reviews, or excerpts, from various publications. There is much popular material here, although the book is problematic for modern readers since it was apparently compiled by editors who were devotees of the simplified spelling movement. There are various diacritical marks for vowel sounds; and orphan becomes orfan, roughly becomes rufly, triumph becomes triumf, and view becomes vue. Another early guide by the indefatigable Ernest A. Baker is *A Guide to the Best Fiction in English*, published in 1913. There are brief entries on plot, type of novel, and evaluation or description. All books included were published before December 31, 1911, and although it is not comprehensive, it does list both popular and serious works.

Specialized bibliographies of fiction related to gothic and romantic formulas are also of much use in searching out titles and authors. For example, Alice Payne Hackett's series of bestseller lists for the R. R. Bowker Company, issued every ten years, can be very helpful for finding books that were popular in their time and for assessing the periods in which gothic and romantic fiction were especially prevalent in publishing history since 1895. The most recent compilation is *Eighty Years of Bestsellers* by Alice Payne Hackett and James Henry Burke. It lists fiction and nonfiction bestsellers year by year, since 1895, and provides an updated overview of all the bestsellers of the period and several specialized lists on such types of books as mysteries, juveniles, and cookbooks. In the 1977 listing (the most recent), *Gone With the Wind* is the number eleven book on the all-time hardcover bestseller list, as the top fiction book on the list after several cookbooks, Kahlil Gibran's *The Prophet*, and five Dr. Seuss books. The number twelve book on the same list is another romantic novel, Anya Seton's *The Winthrop Woman*, a historical romance of the Massachusetts Bay Colony. R. R. Bowker is also the publisher of a new reference guide that will be updated regularly, *Books in Series in the United States, 1966-1975*. This new tool should prove very useful.

Another exceptionally valuable book, although a frustrating and time-consuming one to use, is W. J. Burke and Will D. Howe's *American Authors and Books, 1640 to the Present*, last updated in 1972. This book lists American authors alphabetically along with fairly complete lists of their books. Although a definitive survey of this book would be endless, it is probably the best source around for "fishing expeditions." A cursory survey of the entries under "A" and "B" produced a lengthy list of women authors whose books sounded as though they might be gothic or romantic. The list led to the stacks of the Library of Congress where many of the books on the shelf, dusty and untouched, turned out to be long-forgotten copies of romantic novels by previously unrecorded authors who wrote in both genres. Of course, a researcher would probably not wish to do a complete survey using this method, and it would not be fruitful to be so comprehensive, but used judiciously, the Burke and Howe volume can at least reinforce perceptions of the pervasiveness of such fiction, and occasionally, turn up significant examples of gothic and romantic fiction that might not be found in any other way.

For the earliest gothic works, mostly British, a facsimile reprint series edited by Devendra P. Varma is helpful. *Gothic Novels* is a series of forty volumes of early works, each with its own introduction by a modern scholar of such fiction. Anyone wishing to examine the roots of the gothic in American fiction could find this series immensely valuable. Since so many gothic novels use historical settings, they sometimes appear in bibliographies of historical novels. Ernest A. Baker's 1914 compilation *A Guide to Historical Fiction* indexes books by period of their settings and mentions many romances. There is an extensive section on America. More recently, Ernest E. Leisy's *The American Historical Novel* is an excellent guide to titles and authors. *American Historical Fiction* (third edition), by A. T. Dickinson, Jr., is an annotated checklist arranged by historical period and including both an author-title index and a subject index. Like the Varma series, bibliographical lists of gothic novels tend to be limited to British examples. The most well known of these is Montague Summer's *A Gothic Bibliography*, although it contains no American titles and is notoriously unreliable. The University of Virginia has a fine collection of original gothic novels, described in Rober Kerr Black's *The Sadleir-Black Gothic Collection*, but again there is no American material. Such bibliographies are of use, however, like the Varma series, in exploring the roots of the genre.

More specialized in a way, but useful, are listings of women authors, although of course not all authors listed wrote gothic or romantic fiction. John Hart's *Female Prose Writers of America*, published in the 1850s, is cited as an important source in Nina Baym's *Woman's Fiction*, one of the best recent critical works in the field. Two separate editions of Grant Overton's *The Women Who Make Our Novels*, published in 1918 and 1928, contain biographical and critical essays on a number of writers who were working during that period. The style is almost obsessively chatty, and the critical evaluations are useless, but the biographical and descriptive material is fine for those authors. Overton mixes serious and popular writers, and there are essays on several authors relevant to this study: Mary Roberts Rinehart, Kathleen Norris, Mary Johnston, Amelia E. Barr, Temple Bailey, Faith Baldwin, Margaret Culkin Banning, Fannie Hurst, and Margaret Widdemer. The second volume is more comprehensive.

Gothic novels bear some relationship to detective and mystery fiction and some bibliographic tools on mysteries include gothics as well. The best of these is Ordean A. Hagen's *Who Done It? A Guide to Detective, Mystery, and Suspense Fiction.* Hagen's listings include a wide variety of gothic romances, usually categorized under suspense. Less useful, although worth checking, is Jacques Barzun and Wendell Hertig Taylor's *A Catalogue of Crime.* Unlike reference guides to mystery stories, reference guides to stories of supernatural terror are rare and have little relationship to women's gothic fiction. One possible exception is Everett F. Bleiler's *The Checklist of Fantastic Literature: A Bibliography of Fantasy, Weird, and Science Fiction Books Published in the English Language.* Its usefulness is hampered, however, because it is almost impossible to browse through this book, although information on novels can be checked if the author's name is previously known.

In the late nineteenth century, much women's fiction with gothic elements was published in dime novels, story papers, and women's sentimental novels. Each of these forms was sometimes published in series by publishers. There is no comprehensive guide to such material and some of the best collections are uncatalogued. However, Quentin Reynolds's *The Fiction Factory,* a history of the publications of Street and Smith, provides much solid information on authors, titles, and bibliographic data. A better bibliographic guide is Albert Johannsen's *The House of Beadle and Adams.* Although neither of these books is devoted exclusively, or even primarily, to gothic or romantic fiction, both contain enough information about particular authors and series that they can be of help. For example, "Bertha M. Clay" was a pseudonym used by Street and Smith authors who wrote a particular kind of women's novel with strong gothic characteristics. Reynolds's book provides information on the series and its authors. A much more simplistic guide to dime novels is Charles Bragin's *Bibliography: Dime Novels, 1860-1964,* a twenty-page pamphlet with a short history of the form and lists of some series. Another good source for titles and authors, although time-consuming to explore, is *Publishers Weekly* advertisements. Especially since the 1960s when the popularity of gothic and romantic fiction began to rise, publishers have featured such novels in full-page ads designed to appeal to booksellers who might stock the books. Changes in trends in the fiction as well as specific titles and authors can be found in this way.

Two additional reference works deserve mention for specialized help. A. G. S. Enser's *Filmed Books and Plays, 1928-1967* lists works made into films, with a film title index, an author index, a change of original title index, and a pseudonym index. This is an essential reference book of its type. Gothic and romantic novels have not usually been filmed, but this book quickly identifies those that have been so adapted and, perhaps more importantly, helps in tracing gothic and romantic films to find their sources. For example, one of the finest women's gothic films, Alfred Hitchcock's *Suspicion*, is based upon Francis Iles's *Before the Fact*, which is not a gothic novel. The formula was manipulated by Hitchcock when he made the film. Daphne du Maurier's *Jamaica Inn* was adapted to film as a costume adventure melodrama. Mary Stewart's *The Moonspinners*, a gothic/romantic blend, was turned by Walt Disney Productions into a juvenile mystery. The second useful specialized book is Richard Newman and R. Glenn Wright's *Index to Birthplaces of American Authors*, organized alphabetically and regionally by states and foreign countries. The guide could help in bibliographical work, location of manuscripts, accurate dating, and regionalized studies.

In addition to traditional bibliographic guides, there are many surveys and critical studies of fiction that include bibliographical and descriptive material on gothic and romantic novels. One of the most useful of these is Nina Baym's *Woman's Fiction: A Guide to Novels by and about Women in America, 1820-1870*. This is a good scholarly study, but it also has bibliographic relevance since it has many long plot descriptions in its chapters on individual authors and it surveys the available bibliographic sources. In some ways, the Baym book supersedes what has been for forty years the major book in the field of women's domestic novels, although one cannot ignore the former book since it is more comprehensive than Baym's. Herbert Ross Brown's *The Sentimental Novel in America, 1789-1860* begins earlier than Baym's book and includes a wider range of authors, although her studies of the women she chose to include are more critically useful than his. However, for bibliographical purposes, Brown is essential. He used information about what books were available to the American reading public through libraries and booksellers during the period and compiled some useful statistical lists of such fiction. Another standard work on the woman's novel in the nineteenth century, Helen Waite Papashvily's *All the Happy Endings*, is less useful for bibliographical purposes than Baym or Brown, although she includes a good list of secondary sources before 1954. These three books demonstrate that the field of gothic and romantic fiction is better documented and studied before 1870 than afterward, since there are no comparable studies—or even lists of novel titles—for later periods.

General histories of American fiction sometimes survey that field broadly and include obscure authors and titles that may be of interest.

Alexander Cowie, for example, in *The Rise of the American Novel*, is very good, especially on Charles Brockden Brown, George Lippard, Isaac Mitchell, and a host of minor gothic and romantic novelists. Arthur Hobson Quinn's *American Fiction: An Historical and Critical Survey* is mostly a collection of plot summaries, but although it is dated, its very pedanticism makes it a fine source for information on obscure or unstudied authors. Edward Wagenknecht's *Cavalcade of the American Novel* has an excellent chapter on women novelists, a fine bibliography, and an informative essay on Mary Johnston. The best single source, however, for novels of the early period is Henri Petter's *The Early American Novel*. Petter includes chapters on "Mystery and Terror" and "The Love Story," thus neatly including both gothic and romantic fiction on their own. The bibliographical sections at the end are excellent, including a section of synopses of early novels, arranged in alphabetical order by title, and three separate bibliographies: novels of the period, sources from the period, and modern criticism.

General histories of popular culture and popular fiction can also be fine bibliographical sources, although Norman Cantor and Michael Wertham's *History of Popular Culture* is too compendious to be of much help. But Russel B. Nye's *The Unembarrassed Muse* is an excellent source of bibliographical information on both primary and secondary sources. James D. Hart's *The Popular Book: A History of America's Literary Taste* mentions a great number of novels, both gothic and romantic, especially in his chapters, "The Power of Sympathy" and "Home Influence." Frank Luther Mott's *Golden Multitudes* is also useful, especially on bestsellers, although it is given to trivia and is now out of date. It has lists of bestsellers and better sellers listed by date of publication; *Golden Multitudes* is now probably a better bibliographical tool than a critical one.

Specialized bibliographies and lists are sometimes available in off-beat places. In 1939, for example, Sister Mary Mauritia Redden published her doctoral dissertation, *The Gothic Fiction in the American Magazines (1765-1800)*, at Catholic University. This is probably the only place where information about gothic stories in American magazines before 1800 is systematically listed. She includes appendixes, magazine lists, a bibliography, and a chronological list of stories. Similarly, between 1925 and 1927, Irving Harlow Hart published four articles in *Publishers Weekly*, "Best Sellers in Fiction During the First Quarter of the Twentieth Century," "The Most Popular Authors of Fiction Between 1900 and 1925," "Fiction Fashions from 1895 to 1926," and "The Most Popular Authors of Fiction in the Post-War Period, 1919-1926." Although Hackett's overall lists of bestsellers are more useful for the long view, these four essays show the profile of gothic and romantic authors' popularity in the first quarter of the century, giving an idea of their relative position in publishing.

Bibliographies of secondary works on American gothic and romantic fiction can scarcely appear until much more critical work than now exists has been done. However, some bibliographies of secondary sources contain relevant information, even if it is mainly useful as background. The standard work on gothic fiction is Dan J. McNutt's *The Eighteenth-Century Gothic Novel: An Annotated Bibliography of Critical and Selected Texts*. Although it is almost entirely devoted to British fiction, the book provides brief annotations of bibliographies and secondary sources including background materials, specialized studies, and other items of interest. It is current through 1971. A companion volume on the gothic after the eighteenth century is in progress. Although the focus in this volume, as in so many others, is on the British manifestations of the form and the serious literary consideration of such works rather than the popular culture aspects of the genre, it is still indispensable.

The emerging field of women's studies has also fostered the development of reference guides, some of which point to materials that either relate directly to gothic and romantic fiction or to information about the primary audience for such books—women. Because women's studies is an interdisciplinary field, a number of fairly good bibliographies and research guides have been published in recent years in an attempt to make materials more accessible to researchers than they otherwise could be. The three volumes of *Women's Work and Women's Studies*, compiled by The Women's Center at Barnard College, provide bibliographical guides to sources in women's studies from 1971 to 1974, year by year, in a large number of academic areas. These volumes also have reports of work in progress. An excellent bibliography of social science materials is the *Research Guide in Women's Studies* by Naomi Lynn, Ann Matasar, and Marie Rosenberg, published for undergraduate students and including a great number of entries to standard works pertaining to women's studies in the social sciences. Carol Fairbanks Myers's *Women in Literature: Criticism of the Seventies* is a bibliography of materials about women in literature, some feminist criticism, biographies of women writers, interviews, and some reviews, covering the period from January 1970 to June 1975. Another useful guide, published in Germany, is Dagmar Loytved's *A Bibliographic Guide to Women's Studies II*. It has an excellent section on women authors, including some Americans, and an unannotated checklist of works by women. Of more limited use is *An Annotated Bibliography of Twentieth-*

Century Critical Studies of Women and Literature, 1660-1800, although it has a fine bibliographical section on Ann Radcliffe that should be of interest to those searching for materials on the influences on early American gothic novels. The volume is edited by Paula Backscheider, Felicity Nussbaum, and Philip B. Anderson. Another basic list of works is Beate Resch's *A Selected Bibliography on Women,* another German work. The most essential of these women's studies guides is Narda Lacey Schwartz's *Articles on Women Writers, 1960-1975: A Bibliography.* This is an excellent checklist of articles in English on more than six hundred women writers, citing both popular and scholarly publications and both popular and serious writers. She includes dissertations as well as essays, and she has many gothic and romantic writers represented. Two other reference works are less directly relevant, but might be checked. Patricia O'Connor, Linda Headrich, and Peter Coveny's *Women: A Selected Bibliography* is a standard list of works about women. Su-Ellen Jacobs's *Women in Perspective: A Guide for Cross-Cultural Studies* is an exhaustive bibliography, concentrating on cross-cultural studies and Third World cultures, but it contains a useful, brief section on literature and also a fine list of other bibliographies relevant to women's studies. One more bibliography in women's studies, Rosemary Kowalski's *Women and Film,* surveys articles on women and film in a variety of fields.

The best single source of information about special collections in libraries that might contain relevant examples of gothic or romantic fiction, especially before 1900, is various editions of *Subject Collections,* a publication of the R. R. Bowker Company. The last two editions, both useful, are the third, Lee Ash and Denis Lorenz's *Subject Collections: A Guide to Special Book Collections and Subject Emphases as Reported by University, College, Public, and Special Libraries in the United States and Canada* (1967), and the fourth, Lee Ash's *Subject Collections: A Guide to Special Book Collections and Subject Emphases as Reported by University, College, Public, and Special Libraries and Museums in the United States and Canada* (1974). The fourth edition has been computerized for easy updating. Although it is possible to identify collections of materials pertaining to major authors in these volumes, the books are also of great value in identifying large collections of dime novels, story papers, and other popular forms of entertainment. Since so many of these collections are uncatalogued and relatively untouched by researchers, the listing in *Subject Collections* may be one of the only indicators of gothic and romantic fiction in special collections. R. R. Bowker is also the publisher of a new reference work that should prove very helpful to researchers; Andrea Hinding's two-volume *Women's History*

Sources: A Guide to Archives and Manuscript Collections in the United States is the first reference guide of its type to survey primary materials relating to women in the United States.

Biographical and bibliographical information on writers of gothic and romantic fiction are sometimes included in standard reference guides. Nina Baym mentioned five major resources that she used in compiling information on authors for her book *Woman's Fiction.* Sources from the nineteenth century included the *National Cyclopedia of American Biography, Appleton's Cyclopedia of American Biography,* and John Hart's *Female Prose Writers of America.* Twentieth-century reference works were the two multi-volume standard bibliographical works, *Dictionary of American Biography* and *Notable American Women.* Another standard reference work, in four volumes, is currently being published by Frederick Ungar. Entitled *American Women Writers,* and edited by Lina Mainiero, the work includes known bibliographical and biographical data about American women writers, living and dead, and contains a brief critical essay about each. *Contemporary Novelists* is a single-volume reference guide to living novelists, now entering its third edition. Each entry is a brief summary of bibliographical data, a complete listing of works, an optional writer's statement on his or her own work, and a signed critical essay by a scholar evaluating the writer's career. Among the writers included is Daphne du Maurier. A similar publication, although more specialized, is the recent *Twentieth Century Crime and Mystery Writers,* which has a format like that of *Contemporary Novelists* and includes several gothic and romantic writers.

Studies of the gothic influence on the early American novel might well begin with an examination of Ann Radcliffe, the British writer most influential on her American contemporaries toward the end of the eighteenth and beginning of the nineteenth centuries. A volume in the Twayne series, *Ann Radcliffe* by Eugene Bernard Murray, offers a standard biographical and critical approach to her work and influence. Another interesting source is a 1923 essay in *Contemporary Review* coinciding with the centennial of her death. S. M. Ellis's "Ann Radcliffe and Her Literary Influence" is an appreciative piece asserting that her two main strengths and influences on other authors were her descriptive abilities and her methods of suggesting horror in her works.

Because of the undeveloped nature of this field of study, there are very few bibliographical sources on individual gothic or romantic writers, although there are some historical, biographical, and critical works, as well as some individual manuscript collections. For Charles Brockden Brown, whose American gothic fiction has popular elements, two bibliographical tools are available: S. J. Krause and Jane Nilset's "A

Census of the Works'' and Robert Hemenway and D. H. Keller's "A Checklist of Biography and Criticism.'' The first American writer of women's romances was Susanna Haswell Rowson. In 1875, Caroline Wells Dall published her appreciative book *The Romance of the Association; or, One Last Glimpse of Charlotte Temple and Eliza Wharton: A Curiousity of Literature and Life*. The book represents some of the features of the "Charlotte cult'' or "Charlotte-mania,'' since the author attempts to provide historical background to prove the "truth'' of Charlotte's story and that of Eliza Wharton in Hannah Foster's *The Coquette*. The standard bibliographical source for Rowson is a publication of the American Antiquarian Society, R. W. G. Vail's *Susanna Haswell Rowson, the Author of "Charlotte Temple": A Bibliographic Study*. Published in 1933, the book contains voluminous bibliographical information about various editions of her books. Since *Charlotte Temple* was so popular for such a long period of time, this study offers an important basis for a literary history of the Charlotte phenomenon. Of course, most of those editions are now virtually unavailable, but it might be noted that the Rare Book Collection of the Library of Congress contains a wide variety of editions of the book in various formats. Elias Nason's *A Memoir of Mrs. Susanna Rowson*, published in 1870, is typical nineteenth-century hagiography. More recent studies are more critical than the earlier ones. William S. Kable's introduction to his *Three Early American Novels* (a book that includes *Charlotte Temple* along with Charles Brockden Brown's *Carwin* and *Wieland*) offers a good basic introduction to Rowson. Ellen B. Brandt's *Susanna Haswell Rowson: America's First Best-selling Novelist* is a serious, heavily researched, chronological biography with a critical analysis of the books and a good bibliography. Two brief scholarly essays on Rowson are also useful. Kathleen Conway McGrath's "Popular Literature as Social Reinforcement'' is a straightforward, somewhat simplistic, approach to the popularity of Rowson's novel. Wendy Martin's "Profile: Susanna Rowson, Early American Novelist,'' is a feminist approach to her and her work. According to Brandt, the largest collection of Rowson material is at the American Antiquarian Society, although the collections of the University of Pennsylvania Rare Book Room, the Pennsylvania Historical Society, the Philadelphia Free Library, the New York Historical Society, and other libraries were also useful to her in working on the biography.

A graduate student at Columbia University in the 1920s published the only thoroughly useful materials relating to Elizabeth Oakes Smith; Mary Alice Wyman's two volumes are entitled *Selections from the Autobiography of Elizabeth Oakes Smith* and *Two American Pioneers: Seba Smith and Elizabeth Oakes Smith*. Elizabeth Oakes Smith's papers can be

found at the New York Public Library. Interest in Catharine Maria
Sedgwick has been much greater than that in many other writers of
the mid-nineteenth century, although her major works are not generally
in print today. In 1871 Mary E. Dewey's *Life and Letters of Catharine
M. Sedgwick* was issued; this remained the standard source, supplemented
by a Catholic University dissertation in 1937, Sister Mary Michael
Welsh's *Catharine Maria Sedgwick: Her Position in the Literature and
Thought of Her Time Up to 1860*, until Edward Halsey Foster's
volume in the Twayne series, *Catharine Maria Sedgwick*. An interesting
recent article is Michael Davitt Bell's "History and Romance Convention
in Catharine Sedgwick's *Hope Leslie*." Bell's *Hawthorne and the
Historical Romance of New England* also contains much good information
on Sedgwick. A brief biography of Sedgwick, along with a few other
women writers, appears in Seth Curtis Beach's *Daughters of the Puritans*,
published in 1905. A dissertation on Sedgwick, cited by Foster as
"especially important as a study of Miss Sedgwick's works in the
traditions of nineteenth-century sentimental literature," is Richard B.
Gidez's 1958 "A Study of the Works of Catharine Maria Sedgwick."
A more recent critical essay, putting her in a cultural context, is
Mary Kelley's "A Woman Alone: Catharine Maria Sedgwick's Spinsterhood
in Nineteenth-Century America," published in *New England Quarterly*.
Sedgwick lived in Stockbridge, Massachusetts, where her papers,
manuscripts, and other memorabilia are to be found in the Stockbridge
Library Association's Sedgwick Family collection. There is also a
collection of Sedgwick letters in the Massachusetts Historical Society's
holdings.

Although Sarah Josepha Hale was not a writer of gothic fiction, as
editor of *Godey's Lady's Book* and a prominent woman of letters in
nineteenth-century America, Hale knew women's literature and women
authors well and she published romantic short stories in her magazine.
Good studies of Hale's career remain to be done, but one might
consult Ruth E. Finley's 1931 book *The Lady of Godey's: Sarah Josepha
Hale* or Isabelle Webb Entrikin's privately printed volume *Sarah Josepha
Hale and "Godey's Lady's Book,"* which contains a good bibliography.
A Harvard undergraduate thesis by Nancy Osterud, "Sarah Josepha
Hale: A Study in the History of Women in Nineteenth-Century America,"
was completed in 1971, but could not be examined for this study.
Less useful is Norma R. Fryatt's *Sarah Josepha Hale: The Life and Times
of a Nineteenth-Century Career Woman*, written for children in an effusive
style. Ann Sophia Stephens, another prominent woman writer who was
the author of the first dime novel, *Malaeska*, has not been the subject
of biographical or critical works, but her letters are now available
in the New York Public Library.

Serious consideration of Lydia Maria Child is long overdue. A 1975 essay by Kirk Jeffrey, "Marriage, Career, and Feminine Ideology in the Nineteenth Century: Reconstructing the Marital Experience of Lydia Maria Child, 1828-1874," is a biographical study, but her fiction has not received full-length treatment. Her papers are in the Hofstra University Library, the Child Correspondence in the Ellis Gray Loring Collection at the New York Public Library, the Lydia Maria Child Correspondence of the F. G. and S. B. Shaw Papers in the Houghton Library at Harvard, and the Child Correspondence in the Schlesinger Library at Radcliffe. In addition to the fine section on Caroline Lee Hentz in Nina Baym's book, an essay by Rhoda C. Ellison, "Mrs. Hentz and the Green-Eyed Monster," is useful. Hentz's diaries and letters are in the Southern Historical Collection at the University of North Carolina. There are also Hentz letters in the Chamberlain Collection of the Boston Public Library.

Another interesting figure was Mrs. Lydia Huntley Sigourney, a nineteenth-century poet. Ann D. Wood's essay, "Mrs. Sigourney and the Sensibility of Inner Space," offers an approach to Sigourney through the psychological perspective of Erik Erikson. Sigourney did not write romantic fiction but her situation was similar enough to that of other women writers of her period that her life is instructive. Also, Wood (who now writes as Ann Douglas) offers consistently the best critical studies of American women who wrote. A curious item, although important, is Nathaniel Hall's *A Sermon. Preached in the First Church, Dorchester, on the Sunday (October 8, 1866) following upon the Decease of Maria S. Cummins.* Published by Riverside Press but distributed privately, this sermon portrays Cummins as a feminine paragon, and it indicates how very important feminine virtues were to women's reputations if those women chose to write. The letters and memorabilia of Mary Jane Holmes are in the Seymour Library in Brockport, New York.

Judging from the number of times she is cited in studies of nineteenth-century female romantic writers, there should be a substantial amount of critical work on the life and career of E. D. E. N. Southworth. However, there is virtually nothing available. The only study is a published dissertation, Regis Louise Boyle's 1939 *Mrs. E. D. E. N. Southworth, Novelist.* The Duke University Library has her papers, totalling 342 items. Mrs. Southworth was so prolific and so popular that it is surprising that a thorough reading and study of her work has not been attempted. No good history of nineteenth-century popular fiction fails to mention her prominently.

Susan Warner and her sister Anna B. Warner, authors separately and together of a number of books, lived on Constitution Island near West Point in the Hudson River. The Constitution Island Association maintains their home and some memorabilia and papers. In 1909

Anna B. Warner published a biography of her sister, *Susan Warner*, who was the more famous of the two, having written (under the pseudonym Elizabeth Wetherell) one of the period's most popular novels, *The Wide, Wide World*. The biography is a long, appreciative book of the type one might expect a sister to write in the Victorian period. In 1936 the Constitution Island Association published a commemorative pamphlet, *Constitution Island*, for the meeting of the Garden Club of America. "Susan and Anna Warner: 'The Brontë Sisters of America' " contains a biographical sketch of the two sisters and some material about their life on the island. In 1976, the association published Dorothy Hurlbut Sanderson's *They Wrote for a Living: A Bibliography of the Works of Susan Bogert Warner and Anna Bartlett Warner*, an annotated bibliography noting all known editions of their works and all known works about the sisters.

Another author who deserves more critical attention is Constance Fenimore Woolson; existing studies indicate that some of her fiction may owe a debt to gothic and romantic conventions. Notable are John Dwight Kern's *Constance Fenimore Woolson: Literary Pioneer* and Rayburn S. Moore's Twayne volume, *Constance Fenimore Woolson*. Woolson's niece, Clare Benedict, collected her short works in *Constance Fenimore Woolson* in 1931; that volume also contains a memoir of Woolson by Henry James. Two published dissertations are the only full-length treatments of two other writers: Elizabeth K. Halbeisen wrote *Harriet Prescott Spofford: A Romantic Survival* and William Perry Fidler wrote *Augusta Evans Wilson, 1835-1909*. Both are basic, if uninspired. Spofford's papers are held by the Historical Society of Pennsylvania and the Essex Institute in Salem, Massachusetts. Helen Hunt Jackson, who wrote *Ramona*, is represented in the collections of the Huntington Library and the Jones Library in Amherst, Massachusetts; the latter collection does not circulate. Amelia Edith Barr's autobiography, *All the Days of My Life: An Autobiography*, offers a long, genealogical compendium with lists of her novels, poetry, and letters. About 150 items of Barr papers are in the Texas State Libraries, Archives Division; the collection is restricted. Mary Virginia Terhune called her reminiscences *Marion Harland's Autobiography* after her pen name.

Mary Johnston was the subject of a 1972 dissertation by Gayle M. Hartley, "The Novels of Mary Johnston." Edward Wagenknecht's "The World and Mary Johnston" was in the *Sewanee Review* in 1936. Her papers are in the University of Virginia Libraries, although there is also some interesting correspondence in the Berg Collection at the New York Public Library on the subject of negotiations for stage versions of some of her novels. Laura Jean Libbey, whose working-girl romances were popular during the late nineteenth century, has not been the subject of critical analysis. Her letters are in the New York Public Library. An interesting dissertation is Claudette Ann Diomedi's "Mary Wilkins Freeman and the Romance-Novel Tradition."

Mary Roberts Rinehart is described or evaluated in a few works, although only recently was there a full-length critical biography, Jan Cohn's *Improbable Fiction: The Life of Mary Roberts Rinehart*. Robert H. Davis's *Mary Roberts Rinehart: A Sketch of the Woman and Her Work* is a brief book that includes essays by Davis, Grant Overton, and Rinehart herself. *The Woman Behind the Door . . . Mary Roberts Rinehart* is a publicity pamphlet for one of her new novels, written by Grant Overton. A more scholarly study is an essay in Russel B. Nye's *New Dimensions in Popular Culture*, Arnold R. Hoffman's "Social History and the Crime Fiction of Mary Roberts Rinehart," surveying her bibliography and offering some critical analysis of her work. Rinehart has also written about herself. A book published by The Writer, entitled *Writing Is Work*, describes how she writes. Her autobiography, originally published in 1931 and updated in 1948, is called *My Story*. Her papers, including four hundred catalogued manuscripts, pictures, memorabilia, interviews, and biographical data, are in the Mary Roberts Rinehart Collection in the Special Collections of the University of Pittsburgh Library. Winifred and Frances Kirkland's *Girls Who Became Writers* is a book written for children, containing biographies of Rinehart. Pearl Buck, Sarah Josepha Hale, and Louisa May Alcott.

Fannie Hurst's *Anatomy of Me* is the only full-length source on this writer. Her papers are in the Olin Library, Washington University in Saint Louis, the Special Collections of the Goldfarb Library at Brandeis University, and the University of Texas Library. Isabella M. Alden's *Memories of Yesterdays* is an autobiography edited by her niece Grace Livingston Hill. Hill, herself a romantic writer, is the subject of Jean Karr's *Grace Livingston Hill: Her Story and Her Writings*. Margaret Widdemer was a member of the New York literary set during the early part of this century; she spent time at the McDowell colony and was friendly with many writers of the day. She shared the Pulitzer Prize for poetry with Carl Sandburg, but she also wrote gothic and romantic novels. A chatty and anecdotal autobiography containing reminiscences of the famous people she knew is *Golden Friends I Had*; the title describes the book's content and tone. An excerpt, *Summers at the Colony*, was published by the Syracuse Library Associates. In 1925 Dorothy Scarborough wrote a brief hagiographic biography of Widdemer.

Kathleen Norris was, along with Rinehart, one of the most popular romantic writers of the early part of the century. In addition to the section on her in the Overton volumes, there is little material on her except for her autobiographical writings, *Noon: An Autobiographical Sketch* in 1925 and *Family Gathering* in 1959. Norris was married to a brother of Frank Norris and her sister married William Rose Benét. Her papers are in the Stanford University Library and an unpublished guide to the manuscripts is available at that library. Frances Parkinson Keyes has written many autobiographical volumes. Her earliest work is *Letters from a Senator's Wife*, chronicling her life in Washington. Her comments in this book on her role as a woman are especially interesting. *Capital Kaleidoscope: The Story of a Washington Hostess* is an autobiography about her Washington years written some years after the first. *Along a Little Way* describes her religious conversion from the Congregational to the Episcopalian to the Catholic faith. *The Cost of a Best Seller* is a reminiscence about her writing, including a discussion of her motives, her travel, her illnesses, and her sacrifices for her work. Even *The Frances Parkinson Keyes Cookbook* contains interesting autobiographical material, since she arranges the sections of recipes according to places she has lived and she intersperses personal data throughout the book. *Roses in December*, her first full-scale autobiography, recounts her life from birth to marriage. The second, *All Flags Flying: Reminiscences of Francis Parkinson Keyes*, is a very long book covering her life from her marriage to about 1932. It was unfinished at her death. Her papers are in the University of Virginia Library.

The manuscripts of Marcia Davenport are in the Manuscript Division of the Library of Congress. There are approximately thirty-five hundred items, including literary manuscripts, galley proofs, press clippings, working drafts, notes, and one hundred items of correspondence with Maxwell Perkins, her editor on her romantic novel, *Valley of Decision* (1942). Faith Baldwin's papers are in the Boston University Library, as are those of Anya Seton and Margaret Culkin Banning. (See Appendix 1.) Two interesting sources for work on Kathleen Winsor are available. The Law Library of the Library of Congress has briefs from the obscenity case filed in Massachusetts against *Forever Amber* (1944). A better Winsor collection, however, is in the Manuscript Division of the New York Public Library. That library holds the Macmillan Archives, containing correspondence and other items on the relationship between Macmillan Company and Winsor, especially during the period of *Forever Amber*. There are materials and correspondence on the editing of that book, biographical data on Winsor, letters from readers protesting the morality of Macmillan in publishing the book, and more data on the court case. The Macmillan Archives are also a major source for the study of Margaret Mitchell, although some of the material has been published in Richard Harwell's *Margaret Mitchell's "Gone With the Wind"* *Letters, 1936-1949.*

There are Mitchell papers in a restricted collection at the Atlanta Public Library, in the Library of Agnes Scott College, and at Boston University and Harvard University. A major biography of Mitchell, by Finis Farr, was published in 1965. *Margaret Mitchell of Atlanta* is a discursive book but it contains interesting material about the publication of the novel and its contemporary reception. To commemorate the twenty-fifth anniversary of the book's publication, Macmillan issued a pamphlet, *"Gone With the Wind" and Its Author Margaret Mitchell.* William Pratt's *Scarlett Fever* is a big picture book recounting the book's success and focusing upon the film version. A scholarly study was done as a master's thesis in 1954. William Carter Pollard's *"Gone With the Wind:* Study of a Best Seller" has a good chapter on the bestseller and a fine bibliography, but it is otherwise routine. A few articles about Mitchell have appeared in scholarly or semischolarly journals. Robert L. Groover's "Margaret Mitchell, the Lady from Atlanta," in the *Georgia Historical Quarterly,* is a basic biography. Other articles include Jerome Stern's *"Gone With the Wind:* The South as America" in the *Southern Humanities Review* and Floyd C. Watkins's *"Gone With the Wind* as Vulgar Literature" in the *Southern Literary Journal.* The Watkins article attacks the novel for its inaccuracy about the South. A different view, more laudatory and appreciative and suggesting that the book is worthy of serious treatment, is "Tara Twenty Years After," by Robert Y. Drake, Jr., in the *Georgia Review.* Dawson Gaillard's *"Gone With the Wind* as Bildungsroman; or, Why Did Rhett Butler Really Leave Scarlett O'Hara?" identifies Scarlett as a representative "new woman" in conflict with the Southern Lady as depicted in Melanie Wilkes. Of course, popular magazines have always featured Margaret Mitchell and her novel on appropriate occasions, especially whenever the film is once more released for a new audience.

There are very few sources for the study of modern gothic writers except for the journalistic approaches discussed in Chapter 6. Eleanor Burford Hibbert was featured in Trevor Allen's "Jean Plaidy's Novelised History" in *Contemporary Review.* An interesting approach to Mary Stewart is provided in Maureen Fries's "Rationalization of the Arthurian Matter in T. H. White and Mary Stewart" in *Philological Quarterly,* but the essay refers to her Arthurian trilogy rather than to her gothic novels. A sensitive and semischolarly analysis of Stewart and her popularity appeared in 1965 in *New Statesman;* F. W. J. Hemmings's "Mary Queen of Hearts" was the first published essay to attempt a literary and formulaic analysis of Stewart's novels.

It is encouraging to realize that even a few of these writers have

been studied, written about, and commemorated. It is even more
encouraging to note that research libraries have preserved the manuscripts
and correspondence of some of them. Although many of these
collections are relatively unexamined, to judge by the paucity of scholarly
studies on individual or related authors, for at least some of these
writers the materials for study are available. As scholars in popular
culture, women's studies, and social history begin to recognize the
significance of women's gothic and romantic fiction for women readers
of two centuries, these collections will surely be utilized. In addition,
there is no question that other authors significant in this study will
emerge from obscurity even as others disappear through neglect and
decay of documentary materials. It is inevitable that an ephemeral form
of popular literature can only be partially preserved, but it is long
past the time when such preservation should be begun.

BIBLIOGRAPHY

Alden, Isabella M. [Pansy]. *Memories of Yesterdays.* Edited by Grace Livingston
    Hill. Philadelphia: J. B. Lippincott, 1931.
Allen, Trevor. "Jean Plaidy's Novelised History." *Contemporary Review* 210
    (March 1967): 122-30.
Appleton's Cyclopedia of American Biography. Edited by James Grant Wilson and
    John Fiske. 7 vols. New York: D. Appleton, 1887-1889. Reprint. Detroit:
    Gale Research, 1968.
Ash, Lee. *Subject Collections: A Guide to Special Book Collections and Subject
    Emphases as Reported by University, College, Public, and Special Libraries
    and Museums in the United States and Canada.* 4th ed., rev. and enl.
    New York: R. R. Bowker, 1974.
_____, and Denis Lorenz. *Subject Collections: A Guide to Special Book Collections
    and Subject Emphases as Reported by University, College, Public, and Special
    Libraries in the United States and Canada.* 3d ed., rev. and enl. New
    York: R. R. Bowker, 1967.
Backscheider, Paula, Felicity Nussbaum, and Philip B. Anderson. *An Annotated
    Bibliography of Twentieth-Century Critical Studies of Women and Literature,
    1660-1800.* New York: Garland, 1977.
Baker, Ernest A. *A Guide to the Best Fiction in English.* London: George
    Routledge, 1913.
_____. *A Guide to Historical Fiction.* New York: Macmillan, 1914.
Barr, Amelia Edith. *All the Days of My Life: An Autobiography. The Red
    Leaves of the Human Heart.* New York: D. Appleton, 1913.
Barzun, Jacques, and Wendell Hertig Taylor. *A Catalogue of Crime.* New York:
    Harper and Row, 1971.
Bateson, F. W., and Harrison T. Messerole. *A Guide to English and American
    Literature.* 3rd ed. New York: Gordian Press, 1976.

Baym, Nina. *Woman's Fiction: A Guide to Novels by and about Women in America, 1820-1870.* Ithaca, N.Y.: Cornell University Press, 1978.

Beach, Seth Curtis. *Daughters of the Puritans: A Group of Brief Biographies.* Boston: American Unitarian Association, 1905. Reprint. Freeport, N.Y.: Books for Libraries Press, 1967.

Bell, Michael Davitt. *Hawthorne and the Historical Romance of New England.* Princeton, N.J.: Princeton University Press, 1971.

———. "History and Romance Convention in Catharine Sedgwick's *Hope Leslie.*" *American Quarterly* 22 (Summer 1970): 213-21.

Benedict, Clare, ed. *Constance Fenimore Woolson.* London: Ellis, 1931.

Black, Robert Kerr. *The Sadleir-Black Gothic Collection: An Address Before the Bibliographical Society of the University of Virginia, University of Virginia Library, 1949.* Charlottesville, Va.: University of Virginia Press, 1949.

Bleiler, Everett F. *The Checklist of Fantastic Literature: A Bibliography of Fantasy, Weird, and Science Fiction Books Published in the English Language.* Chicago: Shasta, 1948.

Books in Series in the United States, 1966-1975. New York: R. R. Bowker, 1977-.

Boyle, Regis Louise. *Mrs. E. D. E. N. Southworth, Novelist.* Washington, D.C.: Catholic University of America Press, 1939.

Bragin, Charles. *Bibliography: Dime Novels, 1860-1964.* Rev. ed. Brooklyn, N.Y.: Dime Novel Club, 1964.

Brandt, Ellen B. *Susanna Haswell Rowson: America's First Best-selling Novelist.* Chicago: Serbra Press, 1975.

Brown, Herbert Ross. *The Sentimental Novel in America, 1789-1860.* Durham, N.C.: Duke University Press, 1940. Reprint. New York: Octagon, 1975.

Burke, W. J., and Will D. Howe. *American Authors and Books, 1640 to the Present.* 1962. New ed. New York: Crown, 1972.

Cantor, Norman, and Michael Wertham, eds. *History of Popular Culture.* 2 vols. New York: Macmillan, 1968.

Cohn, Jan. *Improbable Fiction: The Life of Mary Roberts Rinehart.* Pittsburgh, Pa.: University of Pittsburgh Press, 1980.

Constitution Island Association. "Susan and Anna Warner: 'The Brontë Sisters of America.' " In *Constitution Island.* Compiled for the meeting of the Garden Club of America, 1936.

Contemporary Novelists. Edited by James Vinson. New York: St. Martin's Press, 1972-.

Cotton, Gerald B., and Hilda Mary McGill. *Fiction Guides, General: British and American.* London: Clive Bingley, 1967.

Cowie, Alexander. *The Rise of the American Novel.* 1948. Reprint. New York: American Book Co., 1951.

Dall, Caroline Wells. *The Romance of the Association; or, One Last Glimpse of Charlotte Temple and Eliza Wharton: A Curiosity of Literature and Life.* Cambridge: John Wilson, 1875.

Davis, Robert H. *Mary Roberts Rinehart: A Sketch of the Woman and Her Work.* New York: George H. Doran, 1925.

Dewey, Mary E., ed. *Life and Letters of Catharine M. Sedgwick.* New York: Harper, 1871.

Dickinson, A. T., Jr. *American Historical Fiction.* 3rd ed. Metuchen, N.J.: Scarecrow Press, 1971.

Dictionary of American Biography. Edited by Allen Johnson et al. 10 vols. with 5 supplements and index. New York: Scribner's, 1927-.

Diomedi, Claudette Ann. "Mary Wilkins Freeman and the Romance-Novel Tradition." Ph.D. dissertation, University of Maryland, 1970.

Doyle, Paul A. *Guide to Basic Information Sources in English Literature.* New York: John Wiley, 1976.

Drake, Robert Y., Jr. "Tara Twenty Years After." *Georgia Review* 12 (Summer 1958): 142-50.

Ellis, S. M. "Ann Radcliffe and Her Literary Influence." *Contemporary Review* 123 (1923): 188-97.

Ellison, Rhoda C. "Mrs. Hentz and the Green-Eyed Monster." *American Literature* 22 (November 1950): 345-50.

Enser, A. G. S. *Filmed Books and Plays, 1928-1967.* London: André Deutsch, 1968.

Entrikin, Isabelle Webb. *Sarah Josepha Hale and "Godey's Ladies Book."* Lancaster, Pa.: Lancaster Press, 1946.

Evans, Charles. *American Bibliography: A Chronological Dictionary of All Books, Pamphlets, and Periodical Publications Printed in the United States of America from the Genesis of Printing in 1639 Down to and Including the Year 1820.* 14 vols. New York: P. Smith, 1941-1959. Reprint photocopy, reduced size, 13 vols., no index. Metuchen, N.J.: Mini-Print Corp., 1967-.

Farr, Finis. *Margaret Mitchell of Atlanta.* New York: Morrow, 1965.

Fidler, William Perry. *Augusta Evans Wilson, 1835-1909.* University, Ala.: University of Alabama Press, 1951.

Finley, Ruth E. *The Lady of Godey's: Sarah Josepha Hale.* Philadelphia: Lippincott, 1931. Reprint. New York: Arno, 1974.

Foster, Edward Halsey. *Catharine Maria Sedgwick.* New York: Twayne, 1974.

Fries, Maureen. "Rationalization of the Arthurian Matter in T. H. White and Mary Stewart." *Philological Quarterly* 56 (Spring 1977): 258-65.

Fryatt, Norma R. *Sarah Josepha Hale: The Life and Times of a Nineteenth-Century Career Woman.* New York: Hawthorn, 1975.

Gaillard, Dawson. "*Gone With the Wind* as Bildungsroman; or, Why Did Rhett Butler Really Leave Scarlett O'Hara?" *Georgia Review* 28 (Spring 1974): 9-18.

Gidez, Richard B. "A Study of the Works of Catharine Maria Sedgwick." Ph.D. dissertation, Ohio State University, 1958.

Gohdes, Clarence. *Bibliographical Guide to the Study of the Literature of the United States of America.* 4th ed. Durham, N.C.: Duke University Press, 1976.

"Gone With the Wind" and Its Author Margaret Mitchell. New York: Macmillan, 1961.

Griswold, William M., comp. *Descriptive Lists of American International Romantic and British Novels.* 1891. Reprint. New York: Burt Franklin, 1968.

Groover, Robert L. "Margaret Mitchell, the Lady from Atlanta." *Georgia Historical Quarterly* 52 (March 1968): 53-69.

Hackett, Alice Payne, and James Henry Burke. *Eighty Years of Best Sellers.* New York: R. R. Bowker, 1977.

Hagen, Ordean A. *Who Done It? A Guide to Detective, Mystery, and Suspense Fiction.* New York: R. R. Bowker, 1969.

Halbeisen, Elizabeth K. *Harriet Prescott Spofford: A Romantic Survival.* Philadelphia: University of Pennsylvania Press, 1935.

Hall, Nathaniel. *A Sermon. Preached in the First Church, Dorchester, on the Sunday (October 8, 1866) following upon the Decease of Maria S. Cummins.* Cambridge, Mass.: Riverside Press (privately distributed), 1866.

Hart, Irving Harlow. "Best Sellers in Fiction During the First Quarter of the Twentieth Century." *Publishers Weekly* 107 (14 February 1925): 525-27.

_____. "Fiction Fashions from 1895 to 1926." *Publishers Weekly* 111 (5 February 1927): 473-77.

_____. "The Most Popular Authors of Fiction Between 1900 and 1925." *Publishers Weekly* 107 (21 February 1925): 619-22.

_____. "The Most Popular Authors of Fiction in the Post-War Period, 1919-1926." *Publishers Weekly* 111 (12 March 1927): 1045-53.

Hart, James D. *The Popular Book: A History of America's Literary Taste.* New York: Oxford University Press, 1950. Reprint. Westport, Conn.: Greenwood Press, 1976.

Hart, John. *Female Prose Writers of America.* 1852. Rev. and enl. Philadelphia: E. H. Butler, 1854.

Hartley, Gayle M. "The Novels of Mary Johnston: A Critical Study." Ph.D. dissertation, University of South Carolina, 1972.

Harwell, Richard, ed. *Margaret Mitchell's "Gone With the Wind" Letters, 1936-1949.* New York: Macmillan, 1976.

Hemenway, Robert, and D. H. Keller. "A Checklist of Biography and Criticism." *Papers of the Bibliographic Society of America* 60 (July-September 1966): 349-62.

Hemmings, F. W. J. "Mary Queen of Hearts." *New Statesman* 70 (5 November 1965): 698-99.

Hinding, Andrea, ed. *Women's History Sources: A Guide to Archives and Manuscript Collections in the United States.* 2 vols. Index edited by Suzanna Moody. New York: R. R. Bowker, 1979.

Hoffman, Arnold R. "Social History and the Crime Fiction of Mary Roberts Rinehart." In *New Dimensions in Popular Culture,* edited by Russel B. Nye, pp. 153-71. Bowling Green, Ohio: Bowling Green State University Popular Press, 1972.

Howard, Patsy C. *Theses in American Literature, 1896-1971.* Ann Arbor, Mich.: Pierian Press, 1973.

Hurst, Fannie. *Anatomy of Me.* Garden City, N.Y.: Doubleday, 1958.

Jacobs, Su-Ellen. *Women in Perspective: A Guide for Cross-Cultural Studies.* Urbana, Ill.: University of Illinois Press, 1974.

Jeffrey, Kirk. "Marriage, Career, and Feminine Ideology in the Nineteenth Century: Reconstructing the Marital Experience of Lydia Maria Child, 1828-1874." *Feminist Studies* 2 (1975): 113-30.

Johannsen, Albert. *The House of Beadle and Adams.* 2 vols. Norman, Okla.: University of Oklahoma Press, 1950, 1962.

Kable, William S., ed. *Three Early American Novels.* Columbus, Ohio: Charles E. Merrill, 1970.

Karr, Jean. *Grace Livingston Hill: Her Story and Her Writings.* New York: Greenberg, 1948.

Kelley, Mary. "A Woman Alone: Catharine Maria Sedgwick's Spinsterhood in Nineteenth-Century America." *New England Quarterly* 51 (June 1978): 209-25.

Kern, John Dwight. *Constance Fenimore Woolson: Literary Pioneer.* Philadelphia: University of Pennsylvania Press, 1934.

Keyes, Frances Parkinson. *All Flags Flying: Reminiscences of Frances Parkinson Keyes.* New York: McGraw-Hill, 1972.

———. *Along a Little Way.* New York: P. J. Kenedy, 1940. Reprint. New York: Hawthorn, 1962.

———. *Capital Kaleidoscope: The Story of a Washington Hostess.* New York: Harper, 1937.

———. *The Cost of a Best Seller.* New York: Julian Messner, 1950.

———. *The Frances Parkinson Keyes Cookbook.* Garden City, N.Y.: Doubleday, 1955.

———. *Letters from a Senator's Wife.* New York: D. Appleton, 1924.

———. *Roses in December.* Garden City, N.Y.: Doubleday, 1960.

Kirkland, Winifred, and Frances Kirkland. *Girls Who Became Writers.* New York: Harper and Row, 1933. Reprint. Freeport, N.Y.: Books for Libraries Press, 1971.

Kowalski, Rosemary. *Women and Film.* Metuchen, N.J.: Scarecrow Press, 1976.

Krause, S. J., and Jane Nilset. "A Census of the Works." *Serif* 3 (December 1966): 27-57.

Leisy, Ernest E. *The American Historical Novel.* Norman, Okla.: University of Oklahoma Press, 1950.

Loytved, Dagmar. *A Bibliographic Guide to Women's Studies II.* Berlin: John F. Kennedy–Institute für Nordamerikastudien, Freie Universitat Berlin, 1976.

Lynn, Naomi, Ann Matasar, and Marie Rosenberg. *Research Guide in Women's Studies.* Morristown, N.J.: General Learning Press, 1974.

McGrath, Kathleen Conway. "Popular Literature As Social Reinforcement: The Case of *Charlotte Temple.*" In *Images of Women in Fiction: Feminist Perspectives,* edited by Susan Koppelman Cornillon. Bowling Green, Ohio: Bowling Green State University Popular Press, 1972.

McNutt, Dan J. *The Eighteenth-Century Gothic Novel: An Annotated Bibliography of Critical and Selected Texts.* New York: Garland, 1975.

Mainiero, Lina, ed. *American Women Writers: A Critical Reference Guide from Colonial Times to the Present.* 4 vols. New York: Frederick Ungar, 1979-.

Martin, Wendy. "Profile: Susanna Rowson, Early American Novelist," *Women's Studies* 2 (1974).

Microbook Library of American Civilization. *Author Catalog and Title Catalog.* Chicago: Library Resources, 1972.

Moore, Rayburn S. *Constance Fenimore Woolson.* New York: Twayne, 1963.

Mott, Frank Luther. *Golden Multitudes*. New York: Macmillan, 1947.

Murray, Eugene Bernard. *Ann Radcliffe*. New York: Twayne, 1972.

Myers, Carol Fairbanks. *Women in Literature: Criticism of the Seventies*. Metuchen, N.J.: Scarecrow Press, 1976.

Nason, Elias. *A Memoir of Mrs. Susanna Rowson*. Albany, N.Y.: Joel Munsell, 1870.

National Cyclopedia of American Biography. New York: J. T. White, 1893-.

Newman, Richard, and R. Glenn Wright. *Index to Birthplaces of American Authors*. Boston: G. K. Hall, 1979.

New York Public Library. *Dictionary Catalog of the Henry W. and Albert A. Berg Collection of English and American Literature*. 5 vols. Boston: G. K. Hall, 1969.

————. *Dictionary Catalog of the Rare Book Division*. Boston: G. K. Hall, 1971-.

————, Manuscript Division. *Dictionary Catalog*. 2 vols. Boston: G. K. Hall, 1967.

Norris, Kathleen. *Family Gathering*. Garden City, N.Y.: Doubleday, 1959.

————. *Noon: An Autobiographical Sketch*. Garden City, N.Y.: Doubleday, Page, 1925.

Notable American Women. Edited by Edward T. James, Janet Wilson James, and Paul S. Boyer. 3 vols. Cambridge, Mass.: Harvard University Press, Belknap Press, 1971.

Nye, Russel B. *The Unembarrassed Muse*. New York: Dial, 1970.

————. ed. *New Dimensions in Popular Culture*. Bowling Green, Ohio: Bowling Green State University Popular Press, 1972.

O'Connor, Patricia, Linda Headrich, and Peter Coveny. *Women: A Selected Bibliography*. Springfield, Ohio: Wittenberg University, 1973.

Osterud, Nancy. "Sarah Josepha Hale: A Study in the History of Women in Nineteenth-Century America." Undergraduate thesis, Harvard University, 1971.

Overton, Grant. *The Woman Behind the Door . . . Mary Roberts Rinehart*. New York: Farrar and Rinehart, 1930.

————. *The Women Who Make Our Novels*. New York: Moffat, Yard, 1918.

————. *The Women Who Make Our Novels*. New York: Dodd, Mead, 1928.

Papashvily, Helen Waite. *All the Happy Endings*. New York: Harper, 1956. Reprint. Port Washington, N.Y.: Kennikat, 1972.

Petter, Henri. *The Early American Novel*. Columbus, Ohio: Ohio State University Press, 1971.

Pollard, William Carter. "*Gone With the Wind*: Study of a Best Seller." Master's thesis, Florida State University, 1954.

Pratt, William. *Scarlett Fever*. New York: Macmillan, 1977.

Quinn, Arthur Hobson. *American Fiction: An Historical and Critical Survey*. 1936. Reprint. New York: Appleton-Century-Crofts, 1964.

Redden, Sister Mary Mauritia. *The Gothic Fiction in the American Magazines (1765-1800)*. Washington, D.C.: Catholic University of America Press, 1939.

Resch, Beate. *A Selected Bibliography on Women*. Tübingen: privately printed, 1977.

Reynolds, Quentin. *The Fiction Factory*. New York: Random House, 1955.

Rinehart, Mary Roberts. *My Story*. New York: Farrar and Rinehart, 1931.

————. *My Story: A New Edition and Seventeen New Years*. New York: Rinehart, 1948.

————. *Writing Is Work*. Boston: The Writer, 1939.

Sanderson, Dorothy Hurlbut. *They Wrote for a Living: A Bibliography of the Works of Susan Bogert Warner and Anna Bartlett Warner*. West Point, N.Y.: Constitution Island Association, 1976.

Scarborough, Dorothy. *Margaret Widdemer: A Biography*. New York: Harcourt, Brace, 1925.

Schwartz, Narda Lacey. *Articles on Women Writers, 1960-1975: A Bibliography*. Santa Barbara, Calif.: ABC-Clio, 1977.

Schweik, Robert C., and Dieter Riesner. *Reference Sources in English and American Literature: An Annotated Bibliography*. New York: Norton, 1977.

Stern, Jerome. "*Gone With the Wind*: The South as America." *Southern Humanities Review* 6 (Winter 1972): 5-12.

Summers, Montague. *A Gothic Bibliography*. London: Fortune, 1941. Reprint. New York: Russell and Russell, 1964.

Terhune, Mary Virginia. *Marion Harland's Autobiography*. New York: Harper and Row, 1910.

Twentieth Century Crime and Mystery Writers. Edited by John M. Reilly. New York: St. Martin's, 1980.

Vail, R. W. G. *Susanna Haswell Rowson, the Author of "Charlotte Temple": A Bibliographic Study*. Worcester, Mass.: American Antiquarian Society, 1933.

Varma, Devendra P., ed. *Gothic Novels*. 40 vols. New York: Arno, 1971-.

Wagenknecht, Edward. *Cavalcade of the American Novel*. New York: Holt, Rinehart, Winston, 1952.

_____. "The World and Mary Johnston." *Sewanee Review* 44 (April-June 1936): 188-206.

Warner, Anna B. *Susan Warner*. New York: G. P. Putnam's Sons, 1909.

Watkins, Floyd C. "*Gone With the Wind* as Vulgar Literature." *Southern Literary Journal* 2 (Spring 1970): 86-103.

Welsh, Sister Mary Michael. *Catharine Maria Sedgwick: Her Position in the Literature and Thought of Her Time Up to 1860*. Washington, D.C.: Catholic University of America Press, 1937.

Widdemer, Margaret. *Golden Friends I Had*. Garden City, N.Y.: Doubleday, 1964.

_____. *Summers at the Colony*. Syracuse, N.Y.: Syracuse University Library Associates, 1964.

Women's Center at Barnard College. *Women's Work and Women's Studies*. 3 vols. Vols. 1 and 2: Pittsburgh: KNOW, Inc., 1971, 1972. Vol 3: Old Westbury, N.Y.: The Feminist Press, 1974.

Wood, Ann D. "Mrs. Sigourney and the Sensibility of Inner Space." *New England Quarterly* 45 (1972): 163-81.

Woodress, James. *Dissertations in American Literature, 1891-1955, Supplement, 1956-1961*. Durham, N.C.: Duke University Press, 1962.

Wright, Lyle H. *American Fiction, 1774-1850*. 1939. Rev. ed. San Marino, Calif.: Huntington Library Publications, 1969.

_____. *American Fiction, 1774-1900*. Louisville, Ky.: Lost Cause Press, 1970.

Wright, R. Glenn, comp. *Author Bibliography of English Language Fiction in the Library of Congress Through 1950*. Boston: G. K. Hall, 1973.

_____. *Chronological Bibliography of English Language Fiction in the Library of Congress Through 1950.* Boston: G. K. Hall, 1974.

_____. *Title Bibliography of English Language Fiction in the Library of Congress Through 1950.* Boston: G. K. Hall, 1976.

Wyman, Mary Alice. *Selections from the Autobiography of Elizabeth Oakes Smith.* Lewiston, Maine: Lewiston Journal Co., 1924.

_____. *Two American Pioneers: Seba Smith and Elizabeth Oakes Smith.* New York: Columbia University Press, 1927.

PERIODICALS

Publishers Weekly. New York: R. R. Bowker, 1872-.

CHAPTER 3

Related Genres:
Mystery Stories,
Governess Stories,
Melodrama,
and Film Adaptations

The paucity of critical materials on gothic and romantic writers may lead researchers to seek information from sources on related forms of entertainment. For studies of the more adventurous types of gothic novel, some of the classic works on mystery and detective stories can be useful. In some cases, works of serious literature, such as *Pride and Prejudice* (1813) by Jane Austen, *Jane Eyre* (1847) by Charlotte Brontë and *The Turn of the Screw* (1898) by Henry James, are relevant to women's gothic and romantic fiction. The nineteenth-century governess story has clear parallels to many modern gothic novels. The world of nineteenth-century melodrama often seems to resemble that of women's romantic fiction in its structure and value system, and some major works in the gothic and romantic formulas have been adapted to the stage and the screen. This chapter surveys a few of the most useful related sources of information and also suggests strategies for approaching gothic and romantic fiction through similarities to and differences from other forms of popular entertainment.

Since modern gothic novels are so closely related to certain kinds of mystery novels, some of the criticism in that field can help to define and evaluate women's gothics. Gothic novels share with the classic detective story a setting in a confined world in which societal institutions are relatively ineffective. Gothic novels are often mysteries that occur in families, and that concern a small number of persons—all connected to each other—who include villain, victim, and suspects.

Classic detective stories, especially those written by such authors as Agatha Christie and Dorothy Sayers, abound in similar situations. The world in both formulas is closed and self-contained, often claustrophobic in its effect. It is probably no accident that some of the greatest writers of classic detective stories have been women, for women seem to excel in dramatizing the possibilities inherent in domestic situations.

On the other hand, modern gothic novels are a form distinct from the classic detective story. Many critics of detective stories have promulgated long lists of things that detective writers can and cannot do if they wish to play fair with the reader. For the most part, those lists of prohibited techniques negatively define gothic novels, because for all their mysterious elements, gothic novels follow very few of the strictures imposed on detective stories. Writers and readers of these two formulas are aware of the distinctions, although it is probably safe to suggest that there is some overlapping of audience between gothic novels and the more domestic forms of the classic detective story.

The detective formula relies upon *logic*, or the appearance of logic, for the solution to the mystery, and perhaps no requirement of the formula is more rigorous. The detectives, beginning with Dupin and Sherlock Holmes, are masters of deduction who make startling and extensive conclusions from what appears to be slim evidence. The relationship in the detective story between clue and solution is supposed to be absolute; most of the "rules" purport to insure that the reader is not cheated, that the reader has at least the illusion of a chance to come to the conclusion before the detective does. Of course, unless the story is unsatisfying, the detective always reaches the solution first and then elucidates it to the admiring audience (and the readers). In the detective story, the author simultaneously presents and conceals a puzzle; the solution is found and explained by an authority figure who is not involved in the action except in that way.

Although the solution of a mystery is usually important in the gothic novel, the rules of the detective story are universally broken by gothic writers. The reader is invited to solve the mystery along with the heroine, who sometimes seems to function like a detective, but in a very different relationship from that of the detective novel. The heroine in the gothic novel is vitally involved in the mystery and must solve it to save her own life or that of someone else. She seeks to neutralize danger that is threatening her own well-being; thus, she is personally involved. More importantly, the creation and solution of the puzzle is not the only concern of these novels; and, in fact, it is not their main concern. Sometimes the mystery seems almost incidental to the plot, and at most it might be equal in importance to the love story. The author usually conceals the villain but not with the elaborate ruses used by detective writers. Gothic crimes and villains are important not in themselves, but as part of the human relationships in the story. They usually develop directly out of the novel's domestic concerns. The gothic novel subordinates mystery and detection within a domestic melodrama, and in so doing creates a fictional form in which the rules of the detective story are out of place.

For example, detective writers only rarely present villains who are insane. Since the detective novel is based upon logic, the worthy adversaries—villain and detective—must both be capable of rational thought. The detective must be able at the end of the story to explain the puzzle as the product of a rational motive on the part of the villain. Gothic novels place very little emphasis upon the rationality of the mystery or the villain. Solutions to mysteries are often intuitive— a woman's trait—rather than rational. Intuition probably works as well or better in the face of insanity than would deduction.

Another example of how the forms differ is in the relative importance of murder as the crime. In the detective story, murder is usually central to the plot because it is the crime that excites the most horror and fear; it is the ultimate crime and the one that calls forth the most intense activity to thwart it. In gothic novels, there may be a murder but just as frequently it is the mere threat of murder or other violence that provides the suspense. Whether they include an act of murder or not, all gothic novels share a convention that the real villainy may take any form, as long as it threatens the heroine's actual or potential domestic circle. The threat of danger and disruption seems to provide as much suspense as an actual crime.

Many other such comparisons and contrasts between the detective story and the gothic novel can help to define the form, its requirements, its dynamic, and—by implication—its appeal. The excellent sources on detective fiction, one of the most thoroughly catalogued and analyzed of all popular forms, are often helpful. Although they are, of course, somewhat out of date, two volumes, one written by and one edited by Howard Haycraft, offer a good survey of detective fiction prior to 1940. Haycraft's *Murder for Pleasure* surveys and analyzes detective fiction and, judging from the number of times this volume is cited by other critics, it is a standard source of information. *The Art of the Mystery Story* is a volume of essays edited by Haycraft, including work by a number of eminent critics such as R. Austin Freeman, Willard Huntington Wright, "Judge Lynch," E. M. Wrong, and Dorothy L. Sayers. The two volumes together serve to define the formula and describe its major practitioners up to 1940. The disdain of Haycraft and his contributors toward the work of such writers as Mary Roberts Rinehart is especially relevant to an understanding of the relationships between the formulas. Another good source of similar information is A. E. Murch's *The Development of the Detective Novel.* Published in 1958, it is a literary survey of the genre.

Handbooks for would-be writers of mystery and detective stories, as well as occasional articles in *The Writer* magazine, often illuminate the appeal of some of the most mysterious kinds of women's gothic. An anonymous publication, *Murder Manual: A Handbook for Mystery Story Writers,* contains lists of advice for writers. *Mystery Fiction: Theory and Technique* by Marie F. Rodell offers advice from a long-time writer and editor who is more sympathetic to women's forms of mystery fiction than are many other critics. Sutherland Scott's *Blood in Their Ink: The March of the Modern Mystery Novel* is fairly good for the period before 1950. Another guide is Basil Hogarth's *Writing Thrillers for Profit: A Practical Guide.* H. Douglas Thomson's *Masters of Mystery,* first published in 1931, is another useful survey.

The best volume of modern criticism is John G. Cawelti's *Adventure, Mystery, and Romance,* in which he delineates the formulas for a number of related kinds of popular fiction, including detection and the romance. Positing an approach to formulaic analysis, he demonstrates how a careful reading of popular fiction, taking into account such matters as recurrent patterns and aesthetic effect, can elucidate the place of mass entertainment in culture. Much of this book is devoted to detailed discussion of detective and mystery fiction, but Cawelti also offers sound critical principles for the study of women's fiction. His approach to a definition of the romance is both sensitive and provocative. Two reference books should also be consulted for criticism of detective and mystery fiction, Ordean A. Hagen's *Who Done It? A Guide to Detective, Mystery, and Suspense Fiction* and Jacques Barzun and Wendell Hertig Taylor's *A Catalogue of Crime.*

Some modern gothic writers have derived as much from the spy story, or novel of international intrigue, as from the novel of detection. Two chief characteristics of spy fiction have been appropriated: the precarious position of the protagonist and the chase. Modern gothic writers may begin their novels just as many spy thrillers begin, with an innocent, often apolitical, person being caught in someone else's conspiracy and forced to stay involved. The spy novelist Helen MacInnes uses this as an especially favorite ploy, but her work is clearly closer to spy fiction than to the modern gothic novel. Gothics invariably have a female protagonist and MacInnes almost always uses a man. In most cases, modern gothics have first-person narration (or at least, the story is told from a limited point of view). MacInnes uses third person and her story is never filtered through the single view of an individual woman. Modern gothic writers do not care about politics; even in situations of international intrigue, their political conflicts are often merely a way to pose conflicts between good and evil that rarely rise above the level of caricature. Nazis and Communists, for example, if they appear at all, are villains; and the mere labelling of these characters is enough for the reader to recognize them as such. MacInnes, to the contrary, makes fine distinctions among varieties of political positions.

The convention of the "innocent bystander," however distinct that character may be from the one in spy fiction, is very effective in gothic fiction, for it reinforces the sense of precariousness that is almost essential for such novels to work. It provides a way of removing the heroine from her domestic everyday life, and it assures that the novel will be sufficiently suspenseful. By way of contrast, it is instructive to note that in several recent Helen MacInnes novels the "innocent bystander" has been a man, but one of the government agents with whom he works is a woman. He falls in love with her, but she dies in the final confrontation between East and West. It is tempting to suggest that the sex role reversal works a subtle change in the exigencies of the romantic plot. Unlike the gothic novel, where the female protagonist finally wins through to the domestic bliss she deserves, in these MacInnes novels the woman is from the beginning outside the boundaries of acceptable romantic behavior. Is it possible that the reader's imagination would be offended if the uninvolved male hero not only took lessons in deceptive behavior from a woman but then fell in love with her and married her? The best critical source for the formula of the spy thriller is Ralph Harper's *The World of the Thriller*. It defines the formula exceptionally well, and the modern gothic version of this plot can be contrasted with Harper's configuration.

Gothic and romantic fiction have always been influenced and replenished by works of serious fiction. At least until the end of the nineteenth century, when fiction began to respond to modernism, there was a whole series of novels that drew from and gave back to the more formulaic gothic and romantic modes. Influences on the gothic and romantic can be traced from *Pamela* and *Clarissa* through *The Mysteries of Udolpho*, serious novels all in their own right; another strain derives from Jane Austen, especially in her portrayal of the primacy of the courtship ritual for young women and her depiction of such by-now stock characters as the unhelpful parents (Mr. and Mrs. Bennet in *Pride and Prejudice*) and the unwanted suitor. Other influential works of the nineteenth century include Charlotte Brontë's *Jane Eyre*, William Makepeace Thackeray's *Vanity Fair*, and Henry James's *The Turn of the Screw*. It is beyond the scope of this study to survey critical sources on these and other serious works of fiction, but there are a few sources, especially recent feminist criticism, that have important things to say about such books as *women's* books and, in the process, elucidate some of the patterns of gothic and romantic fiction as well.

Four books of recent feminist criticism are especially helpful in examining the literature written by women in nineteenth-century Britain. None deals more than summarily with American literature and all concentrate upon serious fiction, but each has something to offer in interpretation of popular materials by women. Elaine Showalter's *The Female Tradition in the English Novel: From Charlotte Brontë to Doris Lessing* attempts to tie British women writers together in terms of a shared tradition. Patricia Meyer Spacks's *The Female Imagination* posits a theory about the way women write. Ellen Moers's *Literary Women* is a ground-breaking study, for she begins with the premise that one must read novels written by women without losing sight of the sex of the author. Her long analytical sections on female gothic and female "heroinism" are particularly fruitful for adaptation to analysis of popular fiction. She offers a brilliant rereading of many familiar works (most notably, Mary Shelley's *Frankenstein*) and fine evaluation of less familiar novels. Most recently, Sandra M. Gilbert and Susan Gubar's *The Madwoman in the Attic: The Woman Writer and the Nineteenth-Century Literary Imagination* suggests convincingly that women writers, perhaps especially such relevant writers as Austen and the Brontës, wrote only under the burden of an "anxiety of authorship" since they were so publicly acting in a way that women were supposed to be incapable of doing. Women, they argue, resorted to various stratagems and concealments to make their writing acceptable to the largely male literary establishment. This produced an identifiable female imagination that links these and other writers. For the study of popular gothic and romantic writers, Gilbert and Gubar's chapters on Jane Austen and Charlotte Brontë will be most helpful, but note should also be taken of their contention that Emily Dickinson, although a poet, created in her own life a romantic and claustrophobic gothic novel.

In the nineteenth century, governess novels were a reflection of reality, although they often depicted that reality in a conventional literary manner. Economic hardship for women in England often forced gentlewomen into the governess role, since it was one of the few occupations open to women who wished to preserve a measure of gentility. Nineteenth-century governess stories were much more realistic than their modern gothic counterparts, perhaps because so many of women writers were either governesses themselves (Charlotte and Anne Brontë) or knew governesses. Nineteenth-century writers did not idealize the governess's role and often painted it as unattractive. The nineteenth-century governess existed in an undefined social world somewhere between servants and family. Too genteel to associate with servants, but not lofty enough for the family, governesses lived a lonely, solitary life, eating alone on trays in their bedrooms and belonging nowhere during holidays. Governesses were also supposed to be on the lookout for a husband, as many undoubtedly were, as the only acceptable solution to their problems; mothers, wives, and friends of employing families went to some pains to exclude the governess, to be wary of any unusual male attention to the governess, and to quash even innocent flirting. In addition, the governess was in charge of the children but often had no real control over them and was herself blamed for their misbehavior.

Literature, serious and popular, however, abounds with governesses who make the best of their situation, earn the devotion of the children they care for, and eventually marry the master of the house. This pattern is more usual in the modern gothic novel, some years removed from the time when governesses were common; but even before this century, Jane Eyre and Becky Sharp rose through marriage out of the ranks of impoverished single women, while Henry James acknowledged the validity of the fictional pattern, and extended and exploited it, by reversing it in *The Turn of the Screw*.

Several studies of the governess in fiction are relevant to the use of this conventional figure in gothic novels. Katharine West's *Chapter of Governesses: A Study of the Governess in English Fiction, 1800-1949* is the best survey of the subject. She shows how the social position of real governesses gave rise to fictional ones, and she also categorizes the different kinds of governesses in fiction. Patricia Thomson's *The Victorian Heroine: A Changing Ideal* has an excellent chapter on the governess as a fictional convention. A briefer and useful modern essay on the issue of the status of governesses, from which arises most of the tensions of the plot convention, is M. Jeanne Peterson's "The Victorian Governess: Status Incongruence in Family and Society."

There are, of course, other influences on gothic and romantic fiction, but the mystery, the spy thriller, and the governess convention are probably the most fruitful to examine. A different approach to these women's novels is to compare them to other media. Unlike many other formulas of popular fiction, such as the detective story, the Western, and the spy thriller, gothic and romantic novels have not been systematically adapted for the theater and for movies. However, the relationship between different versions of such stories in different media serves to clarify some of the characteristics of these stories. In some cases, the novels have been adapted and the result, when compared to the original book, is also instructive. Although some nineteenth-century gothic and romantic novels may have served as the basis for stage plays, it is uncertain. What is clear is that there were strong parallels between the world view of such novels and that of the stage melodrama. The theater in America in the nineteenth century thrived upon adaptations of some popular novels, notably two of the most successful and long-running plays of the period, *Uncle Tom's Cabin* and *Rip Van Winkle*. Research may demonstrate in the future that gothic and romantic novels had a direct influence on stage melodrama; but, in the absence of critical studies, it is possible to compare what is known about each form and to see the relationships in terms of plots, conventions, and values. Hollywood's search for material to adapt has led some producers and directors to women's gothic or romantic novels, but such adaptations have been relatively rare because film makers are wary of the potential of such works to attract a mass audience. The audience for gothic and romantic fiction is self-selected (and primarily female) and since the books do not usually attract the attention of male readers, they might not attract a male audience in film.

However, the most problematic factor in adaptation of gothic or romantic novels to stage and screen is the difficulty of translating such books without substantial change in the narrative strategy. The formulas depend intensely upon the very narrative convention that is most difficult for the theater and the movies to use. Virtually evey gothic or romantic novel is told in the first person, or in the limited third-person mode, by the female protagonist. The drama of this fiction is interior and psychological, and its very structure depends upon the identification between female protagonist and female reader. These novels, no matter what their plot outlines may be, relate a story that can be fully articulated only in the mind. They ask (or imply) the question of whether this hero and this heroine will finally be united. All dramatic events in the fiction work toward the resolution of this question. It is relatively simple to portray that relationship when the narrative is presented from the point of view of the female protagonist. It is much more difficult in a "third person" medium such as theater or film. However, in the hands of such skilled directors as

Alfred Hitchcock, it has been accomplished. Some other versions of these stories have changed them so substantially in adaptation that the important tension of gothic or romantic fiction is removed.

However, adaptation is not the only way to approach the problem, for it is clear that, despite changes in plot and point of view, stage plays and films have often shared the conventions of gothic and romantic fiction. David Grimsted in *Melodrama Unveiled* describes the world view of the stage of melodrama in the nineteenth century; there are several significant common elements between melodrama and women's romantic fiction. It was common for the melodrama to combine a love story with an adventurous mystery in which an evil villain had designs on the person or property of an innocent girl, who was saved by her potential lover or husband. Melodrama, while serving up adventure to its audience, affirmed the primacy of love. Another shared convention is the set of stock characters and situations relating to fathers, mothers, and daughters. As early as *Clarissa Harlowe*, fathers appeared in some romantic fiction as heavy-handed authority figures trying to force their daughters into loveless marriages. However, in the melodrama, as in most gothic and romantic novels, the father is a sympathetic figure, although he may be authoritarian. Grimsted points out that the father in melodrama often provided the moral center to the play, moralizing and lecturing, often on chastity, and setting up a conflict between the heroine's love and her duty. The mothers, on the other hand, were much less attractive. They were frequently too eager to force their daughters into marriage; they were social climbers who never could understand how the daughter could be attracted to the unpretentious hero. In the melodrama, the machinations of such mothers were foiled. In some cases, the mothers were not venal or mean, they were merely obtuse and silly, unable to advise their daughters appropriately on the course of their future lives. This pattern is exemplified in fiction by Elizabeth Bennet's parents in Jane Austen's *Pride and Prejudice*. Mr. Bennet is respected by his daughters but helpless to improve their prospects; Mrs. Bennet, however, urges upon them behavior that is certain to harm their chances of making good matches.

In gothic and romantic novels through two centuries, mothers may not be such a dramatic hindrance to the fortunes of their daughters as they were in the melodrama, but are often absent or ineffective. Many authors "kill off" the heroine's mother before the daughter reaches adulthood and conflict. Fathers may be absent also, but they occasionally serve a kind of symbolic function as the moral center of the plot even if they are not directly involved in the action. For example, in Maria Susanna Cummins's *The Lamplighter*, Gertie spends much of her life wondering what her father had been like, only to discover at the end of a very long book that she has known him all along. He has secretly looked out for her and offered timely advice throughout the book. In only a very few of the modern gothic and romantic novels is the father a moral paragon in contrast to a silly, venal mother, but modern novelists do not so much change the pattern as evade it by writing about a heroine whose parents are either dead or unavailable to her for help. Such women, forced to act on their own, are free to have adventures and to make decisions on their own. In some of the modern gothic novels, most notably those of Phyllis Whitney, the plot centers upon a daughter's search for the truth about her parents. The shared conventions of melodrama and gothic fiction are crucial to the development of this plot pattern. In this century, the stage melodrama has changed its form, so that the relationships between it and the gothic novel are not so close. On the other hand, in the modern gothic novel, and occasionally in more domestic romantic fiction, some of the old value patterns and shared assumptions of melodrama and gothic fiction are still viable. The best critical and descriptive source for melodrama is Grimsted, although Frank Rahill's *The World of Melodrama* could also be consulted. There is very little information about adaptations of gothic and romantic novels to the stage. (See Appendix 1 for a discussion of the materials available in the New York Public Library.)

In the case of film, however, the problems of adaptation are both more pointed and more revealing of the formulaic imperatives of gothic and romantic fiction. In one notable case, director Alfred Hitchcock adapted a straightforward third-person suspense story to the screen, and by making a few strategic changes he created a gothic mystery of the "suspicious husband" plot type so commonly employed by Victoria Holt and other gothic writers. The case is significant; for it suggests that point of view and sensibility, working together, may be the most significant defining factors of gothic and romantic fiction for women. If the story is told from a first-person female point of view (or at least a limited female point of view) and all action is subordinated to its effect on the love relationship, the story is recognizably gothic or romantic. If the plot elements are removed from this focus, the tensions of the story must derive from other plot elements and the story is no longer female gothic or romantic.

Hitchcock's film was *Suspicion* (1941), adapted from a British novel by Francis Iles, entitled *Before the Fact* (1932). The novel concerns a young wastrel who is almost too charming. Always in need of money, he marries a mousy country girl who, he believes, can support him. When his needs outrun her means once again, he kills her by giving her poison. She knows what he is doing, but acquiesces, and he is not caught. The book is written in the third person.

Hitchcock's version shifts the focus more directly to the wife, played by one of his favorite stars, Joan Fontaine, who had worked for him in *Rebecca* (1940) the previous year. Fontaine, as Lina, meets her future husband, played by Cary Grant, on a train. She is a sheltered girl who wears glasses, reads constantly, and dresses drably. Johnny is a typical Cary Grant character, suave and debonair. He pursues her outrageously and finally, in an entirely irrational and emotional manner and against the objections of her parents, Lina decides to marry him. Up to this point, Hitchcock presents the story faithfully from the outside, but from this point on, he moves closer and closer to Lina's sensibility, succeeding in many scenes in showing us her emotions and imaginings about Johnny through cinematic technique. Johnny's behavior becomes more suspicious as Lina begins to see through his lies. She makes excuses, but the suspicions recur. At the end of the film, Lina is convinced that Johnny is a murderer and that he is trying to kill her. In the end, however, the film concludes as do many modern "suspicious husband" gothics. The suspicions are wrong; Johnny has been profligate but not evil. He has been venal but he loves her. She pleads to help him straighten out his life and he apologetically acquiesces.

There has been critical controversy over this ending and, in fact, it does not work very well. Whether the Hollywood system or Hitchcock himself was responsible, the ending seems implausible and abrupt. Still, Hitchcock's achievement in suggesting the first-person point of view visually without resorting to voice-over narrative brings this film as close to gothic/romantic sensibility as a film can probably be.

The tendency in most adaptations of gothic or romantic material is not to choose the daring ploy of Hitchcock but to turn the novels into straight adventure films by adding scenes that could be appreciated by a male audience, de-emphasizing the love story, and shifting the narrative center from the woman's mind to an omniscient, all-seeing camera. Two gothic novels that have received such treatment are Daphne du Maurier's *Jamaica Inn* (1936) and Mary Stewart's *The Moonspinners* (1962). *Jamaica Inn* is a story set in Cornwall about a young orphan who finds herself in the midst of a den of smugglers. The film version was Hitchcock's last made in Britain before he moved to Hollywood. Produced in 1939, the film stars Charles Laughton, Maureen O'Hara (unknown at the time), and Emlyn Williams. Inevitably, a character (especially a villain) played by Laughton would overshadow a character played by Maureen O'Hara, and much of the interest in this film shifts to the smugglers and their adventures and away from the innocent girl. The film lacks the woman's perspective that is so essential to gothic/romantic fiction. In this film, unlike *Suspicion*, the audience knows more than the heroine does, including the identities of the villains. In the case of Stewart's *The Moonspinners*, the adaptation by Walt Disney Productions turns a women's gothic romance into a children's adventure story. The heroine of the novel is young, probably about twenty-two, but as played by Hayley Mills in the Disney version, she seems much younger. The hero in the book is older, probably in his late twenties, but as played by Peter McEnery, he also seems too young for romance. This juvenilization also effectively de-emphasizes the love story and brings the adventure to the fore, destroying the gothic and romantic sensibility of the original.

Adaptations of gothic and romantic fiction often distort the originals in two ways: adventure sequences are emphasized over the love story so as to appeal to a wider audience, and the point of view or center of consciousness shifts outward away from the mind of the female protagonist, who becomes merely another character in the story. There are exceptions, however, and the whole relationship between these originals and their stage and screen versions helps to define the characteristics of the genre.

Although the literature on film is immense and growing, only a few sources are actually very helpful in looking at adaptations of gothic and romantic fiction. A good starting place is the chapters on film in Russel B. Nye's *The Unembarrassed Muse*, both for his breadth of coverage and for his careful avoidance of pejorative analysis of popular works. For the background of the film industry in the United States, Robert Sklar's *Movie-Made America* is useful. Two bibliographical sources are essential. For locating adaptations from book (or play) to screen, the best source is A. G. S. Enser's *Filmed Books and Plays, 1928-1967*. This is a reference book, containing a film title index, an author index, a change of original title index, and a pseudonym index. The work identifies the original publisher of the book and the company that produced the film. Another, different, bibliographical source is a reference book by Rosemary Kowalski entitled *Women and Film*. This is a collection of entries on books, articles, and essays on the general subject of women and film. It is comprehensive and valuable.

Molly Haskell, in her fine study *From Reverence to Rape: The Treatment of Women in the Movies*, notes that love as experienced by women is a devalued commodity in films. "That love is women's stuff is a hoary, Anglo-Saxon idea, devolving from the (American) tough guy and (British) public school etiquette that to show emotion is bad form, a sign of effeminacy, and that being tender in love is the equivalent of doing the dishes or darning socks."[1] In such a schema, it is no wonder that novels promoting a woman's point of view would undergo significant change in emphasis when adapted for a medium that has to sell tickets to members of both sexes.

Haskell, however, identifies one type of film, called the woman's film, that sounds very much like gothic and romantic fiction, even though the point of view may be different. She says that the woman's film is a middle-class genre, defining middle class as a "state of mind and a relatively rigid moral code."[2] Women have a limited range of options in society, she suggests, each of which works to make her dependent upon a man. "She . . . feels bound to adhere to a morality which demands that she stifle her own 'illicit' creative or sexual urges in support of a social code that tolerates considerably more deviation on the part of her husband. She is encouraged to follow the lead of her romantic dreams, but when they expire she is stuck."[3] Even stars like Katharine Hepburn and Joan Crawford, who projected strong images in their films, starred in films that ended with female capitulation to male dominance through marriage. But at least in those films, women were more active, more competitive, and somewhat more interesting than the heroines of most adaptations of gothic or romantic novels, with their stance of innocent victim, could possibly be.

Only in the hands of a master like Hitchcock or David Lean could the full cinematic potential of these novels be realized. It is probably also true that a gifted director must have a star who can project the sort of interesting victimization that Hitchcock was able to summon from Joan Fontaine and Ingrid Bergman. In Fontaine's gothic films, especially *Jane Eyre*, *Rebecca*, and *Suspicion*, she had to portray vulnerability without becoming so colorless as to be uninteresting. She has an expressive face and was able to capture the feel of the gothic heroine in each of these films. James Parish suggests, "Her affinity for vulnerableness would become the essential quality of Joan's 1940s star image."[4]

In *Rebecca* (1940), Hitchcock was less daring technically than he was to be in *Suspicion*. The adaptation is very close to the original, even to the detail that the narrator and protagonist has no name. Hitchcock uses voice-over narration in this film to keep the point of view with the heroine, so that the audience does not know until late in the film, as in the book, what the true story of the past had been. As for *Jane Eyre*, Geoffrey Wagner argues that the book was diminished by the film's indebtedness to *Rebecca*, surely an irony since the book, *Rebecca*, is so indebted to Brontë's novel. Wagner says that all the personality and feistiness and strength of Brontë's Jane dissipates into another of Fontaine's colorless victims. "One must strongly censure someone for the total and quite unnecessary suppression of Jane's intellect in the role played by Joan Fontaine. It is highly likely that the nature of the star compounded this misinterpretation, for Fontaine was playing meek-and-mild plain Janes one after another at this time, including, opposite a moustached Laurence Olivier, a very similar role in *Rebecca*, itself a bold plagiarism of *Jane Eyre*."[5] Despite these strictures, however, Fontaine projects in all of these films the kind of insecurity in a precarious world, the aptitude for victimization, and the purity necessary to the gothic heroine. The adaptations in which she starred were more faithful to the originals than were any others.

Ingrid Bergman played similar roles, although her pictures were not always adaptations. Bergman was once described in a way that suggests many gothic heroines of recent years. "Bergman embodies the most human, provocative, and cherishable qualities that we ordinarily associate with women at their most womanly—innate strength overcoming a passing vulnerability, and an untarnished beauty that inspired in both men and women a pride in human dignity."[6] The quote is from Curtis F. Brown's *Ingrid Bergman*, a part of the Pyramid Illustrated History of the Movies series. The book's most useful feature for the researcher is its plot summaries of all of Bergman's films.

Bergman's characters are usually more dynamic than those of Joan Fontaine, but they still project the vulnerability of the gothic heroine. Two of her films, neither adapted from a gothic original, show particular characteristics of the formula. In *Spellbound* (1945), Bergman played a psychiatrist in love with an imposter whose amnesia makes him helpless in the face of suspicions that he is a murderer. Interestingly, the Bergman character, who is competent, tough, and antiromantic at the beginning of the film, makes her assessment of the man's character in exactly the same way as a gothic heroine would. She tells herself that she could not feel that way about an evil man. Ironically, her willingness to commit herself to him and risk her career on him also makes her a better doctor since she lets her womanly intuition supplement her training.

Spellbound and her next film, *Notorious* (1946), were both directed by Hitchcock. In *Notorious*, Hitchcock took an espionage plot and gave it a woman's perspective. Bergman is pushed into spying, much as women in some modern gothic romances are. The audience knows little more than she does until near the very end. Her spymaster, played by Cary

Grant, is a tough guy, unemotional and so controlled that there is no way of knowing what he is thinking. He resembles the undemonstrative, enigmatic heroes of most gothic and romantic novels. He loves her but refuses to tell her so because it might cause her to stop working for him. But it is her perspective and the female value system that control most of the film. One critic commented: "Although *Notorious* seems to be a spy melodrama, in fact it is not. The espionage activities are really Hitchcock's MacGuffin, his ubiquitous pretext for more serious, abstract issues. Here, the serious issue is one of common humanity—the possibility of love and trust redeeming two lives from fear, guilt and meaninglessness."[7]

After these two films, Bergman played other similar roles for Hitchcock and others, including the wife-victim in *Gaslight*, the heroine in *Under Capricorn* (which one critic suggested "tried to repeat the haunting formula of *Rebecca*"[8]), and the nameless governess in a fine NBC-TV version of *The Turn of the Screw* in 1959, for which she won an Emmy.

Scholarly evaluation of the work of actresses such as Joan Fontaine and Ingrid Bergman is yet to be done. Most commentary upon their work occurs in books aimed at fans and film historians; such is Ronald Bowers's *The Selznick Players*, which has long sections on both actresses but is hagiography rather than criticism. Arlington House publishers seems to specialize in big, glossy picture books for fans. Two of these, *The RKO Gals* and *Hollywood's Great Love Teams*, are by James Robert Parish. *The RKO Gals* is chatty, but it has fairly good sections on the careers of Fontaine and Maureen O'Hara. *Hollywood's Great Love Teams* is a massive popular reference book with filmographies, synopses, and photos. Another Arlington House book, Ted Sennett's *Lunatics and Lovers: A Tribute to the Giddy and Glittering Era of the Screen's "Screwball" and Romantic Comedies*, is also heavy on plot, emphasizing comedies (not gothic or romantic films), but it does have some material on the Cinderella myth in the movies.

Critical work on Hitchcock abounds and some of it offers good theoretical speculation on how and why Hitchcock developed the special sensibility toward a certain type of woman's role relevant to the gothic. Of these, one of the most useful is Robin Wood's *Hitchcock's Films* in which he offers close critical analyses of a number of Hitchcock's major works. Another useful source is Maurice Yacowar's *Hitchcock's British Films*, containing especially good sections on *Jamaica Inn* and *The Lady Vanishes*. Fine critical analysis is found in Donald Spoto's *The Art of Alfred Hitchcock: Fifty Years of His Motion Pictures* with long, excellent analyses of each film. Less useful and less scholarly are several other sources. George Perry's *Hitchcock* is a glossy illustrated book that is mostly description. Raymond Durgnat's *The Strange Case of Alfred Hitchcock; or, The Plain Man's Hitchcock* is an odd analysis of each of Hitchcock's films. Durgnat delights in challenging the interpretations of other critics and second-guessing Hitchcock as when he restructures *Suspicion* by providing three possible endings, showing how the film could have been changed to accommodate each of them. Peter Bogdanovich's *The Cinema of Alfred Hitchcock* consists mainly of interviews with Hitchcock and brief comments on most of the films. An out-of-the-way source of limited value is Renee Ruben's *"Jamaica Inn": The Story of the Film*, issued by "The Mayflower" Pictures Corporation, Ltd., to coincide with the film's release. It is an eleven-page pamphlet with a simple plot description for the film.

Other films adapted from gothic and romantic sources include *Forever Amber*, made by Otto Preminger and starring Linda Darnell; *Dragonwyck*, adapted from Anya Seton's novel of the same name; and *The Valley of Decision*, made from Marcia Davenport's novel and starring Gregory Peck and Greer Garson. Two adaptations of Henry James's *The Turn of the Screw* are also significant. The novel, of course, is most ambiguous about the existence of the ghosts, although the first-person narration and the characteristics of the heroine show the clear relationship between the book and the gothic romance. In the two adaptations, the ghosts appear on the screen, so the ambiguity about the governess's perception is resolved. The first, *The Turn of the Screw*, was made by NBC-TV with Ingrid Bergman in 1959. The second, entitled *The Innocents*, was a feature film starring Deborah Kerr, adapted in its turn from a stage version of the same name. Jeanne Thomas Allen's *"Turn of the Screw and The Innocents*: Two Types of Ambiguity" discusses the latter adaptation.

Although it is not an adaptation, one of the best examples of a gothic/romantic story in recent film history is David Lean's *Ryan's Daughter* (1970). One of Lean's critics, Gerald Pratley, says: "This form of romance, usually contemptuously dismissed as 'women's magazine' material, is hard to describe and hard to film without making it seem trite and sentimental. But such is Lean's skill at interpretation in visual terms, that audiences are never manipulated by sentimentality or melodrama."[9]

Ryan's Daughter is the story of a girl growing up in a wild and isolated part of the west of Ireland during the years of the troubles after the Easter Rebellion of 1916. Rosie Ryan, played by Sarah Miles, is a pretty girl and a dreamer, dissatisfied with her mundane life as the daughter of a widowed publican but also ignorant of the world outside her small but spectacularly beautiful corner of Ireland. Rosie's romantic dreams derive partly from the inspiration offered by the local schoolmaster, played by Robert Mitchum. She fancies herself in love with him, although it is clear to the audience that he is not what she thinks he is. In fact, he himself tells her so, saying: "I only told you about Beethoven, Ireland, and Cap'n Blood. I'm not one of those fellows myself." But Rosie will not listen and she convinces him to marry her. Of course, her dreams are not fulfilled in the marriage and within a short time she is having an affair with a handsome but troubled British officer stationed in the region. At this point, the adventure aspects of the plot begin to take over and become thoroughly intertwined with Rosie's story as she is assumed by the townspeople to be a collaborator with the hated British.

Most important, however, in the similarity of *Ryan's Daughter* to gothic and romantic fiction is Lean's treatment of female sexuality. Lean focuses on faces to show feelings, much as Hitchcock had done earlier; and, in two parallel love scenes, he uses the technique to make the same statement about sex and love that is made in innumerable women's novels. Many of these novels also employ parallel scenes that serve to define female sexuality and to identify the hero as well, most notably in Anya Seton's *Katherine*. Rosie's wedding night is a great disappointment to her and we begin to see the disintegration of her romantic dreams at that point. The schoolmaster, in one brief, perfunctory sex act, fails to satisfy her; Lean focuses directly on her face throughout to show her hurt, disappointment, and pride. Rosie, identifying her husband as her "true love," had assumed that sex would be automatic and fulfilling; she requires him to be a romantic hero and he is incapable of it. After that scene, Lean shows in Rosie's eyes constant small disappointments which, because she does not understand how unreal her dreams are, she interprets as rejection.

When she falls in love with the British officer, she begins to believe in the dreams again because their first encounters, sexual and otherwise, are so overwhelming. She cannot resist her attraction to him, and the contrast between the expression on her face with him and that with her husband—underscored by Lean's fine camera work—tells the story. The film is worth examining, even though it is not a pure example of women's gothic or romantic fiction, because of the use of that plot element of the sexual test, so common in romantic fiction, often in very subtle rather than overt ways. One of the ways that a reader knows that a marriage—usually a marriage of convenience—is doomed to failure is if the heroine is dissatisfied in the sexual relationship. These books are never explicit about such matters, but in subtle ways the reader becomes aware of a problem emanating from the marriage bed. True love, on the other hand, is signalled by an overwhelming, magical—almost dreamlike—attraction, such as the one Lean portrays in this film.

Lean does not rely totally upon romantic conventions for this film, for the officer commits suicide and Rosie is punished by her neighbors. She is shown leaving the community with her husband, who will take her to Dublin and set her up on her own, he says, so that she is no longer tied to a husband she does not love. The film ends ambiguously. But surely Lean is relying on cues and value structures from women's fiction in making this film, just as he relies on techniques similar to Hitchcock's in portraying female sensibility.

Gerald Pratley's *The Cinema of David Lean* has an excellent section on *Ryan's Daughter* with a discussion of its affinity to women's fiction. Alain Silver and James Ursini in *David Lean and His Films* take an auteur theory approach, with a section on *Ryan's Daughter* emphasizing the images of the film and how they underscore the emotional content. They do a poetic analysis of the film, referring to Rosie's yearning, under the influence of her reading of popular fiction, for the man of her dreams.

Of course, much has been written on the making of *Gone With the Wind*, that perennially favorite romantic film, but one might wish to consult, especially, Gavin Lambert's two-part essay "Making of *Gone With the Wind*," a discussion of how David Selznick produced the film. A glossy book by William Pratt, *Scarlett Fever*, is about the phenomenon of the film's popularity. It includes a number of black and white pictures.

Relevant works of film criticism and theory include George Bluestone's classic study, *Novels into Film*, and Geoffrey Wagner's *The Novel and the Cinema*, both of which concentrate upon film adaptation. John Kobal's *Romance and the Cinema* has an interesting chapter on the adaptation of romances to film. Some good work has also been done on women and film. For a comprehensive listing, the Kowalski bibliography gives the major sources. But Molly Haskell's *From Reverence to Rape* is the best history of images of women in the movies. Brandon French's book, *On the Verge of Revolt: Women in American Films of the Fifties*, has as its subject the double message of such films.

On the surface, fifties films promoted women's domesticity and inequality and sought easy, optimistic conclusions to any problems their fictions treated. But a significant number of movies simultaneously reflected, unconciously or otherwise, the malaise of domesticity and untenably narrow boundaries of the female role. By providing a double text, which contradicted itself without acknowledging any contradiction, that is, by imitating the culture's schizoid 'double-think'—they documented the practical, sexual, and emotional transition women were undergoing beneath the threshold of the contemporary audience's conscious awareness.[10]

Another study of women and the movies, a reader compiled for college writing classes, also contains some useful material. Marcia McCreadie's *The American Movie Goddess* is an elementary, although helpful, source.

Looking at gothic and romantic fiction through the prism of studies of related genres and adaptations cannot provide direct analysis, but as a starting place for theoretical considerations, it is valuable. The recognition of the differences between formulas and the consideration of such aesthetic problems as the qualitative differences between *Jane Eyre* and modern "governess gothics" can only give rise to more precise critical distinctions and definitions and more profound and meaningful critical analyses.

NOTES

1. Molly Haskell, *From Reverence to Rape: The Treatment of Women in the Movies* (New York: Holt, Rinehart and Winston, 1974), p. 157.

2. Ibid., p. 159.

3. Ibid., p. 160.

4. James Robert Parish, *The RKO Gals* (New Rochelle, N.Y.: Arlington House, 1974), p. 480.

5. Geoffrey Wagner, *The Novel and the Cinema* (Rutherford, N.J.: Fairleigh Dickinson University Press, 1975), pp. 345-46.

6. Curtis F. Brown, *Ingrid Bergman* (New York: Pyramid Publications, 1973), p. 14.

7. Donald Spoto, *The Art of Alfred Hitchcock: Fifty Years of His Motion Pictures* (New York: Hopkinson and Blake, 1976), p. 162.

8. Brown, *Ingrid Bergman*, p. 93.

9. Gerald Pratley, *The Cinema of David Lean* (New York: A. S. Barnes, 1974), p. 206.

10. Brandon French, *On the Verge of Revolt: Women in American Films of the Fifties* (New York: Frederick Ungar, 1978), p. xxi.

BIBLIOGRAPHY

Allen, Jeanne Thomas. *"Turn of the Screw* and *The Innocents*: Two types of Ambiguity." In *The Classic American Novel and the Movies*, edited by Gerald Peary and Roger Shatzkin. New York: Frederick Ungar, 1977.

Barzun, Jacques, and Wendell Hertig Taylor. *A Catalogue of Crime*. New York: Harper and Row, 1971.

Bluestone, George. *Novels into Film*. Berkeley: University of California Press, 1957.

Bogdanovich, Peter. *The Cinema of Alfred Hitchcock*. New York: Museum of Modern Art Film Library (distributed by Doubleday), 1963.

Bowers, Ronald. *The Selznick Players*. New York: A. S. Barnes, 1976.

Brown, Curtis F. *Ingrid Bergman*. Pyramid Illustrated History of the Movies. New York: Pyramid Publications, 1973.

Cawelti, John G. *Adventure, Mystery, and Romance: Formula Stories As Art and Popular Culture*. Chicago: University of Chicago Press, 1976.

Durgnat, Raymond. *The Strange Case of Alfred Hitchcock; or, The Plain Man's Hitchcock*. London: Faber and Faber, 1974.

Enser, A. G. S. *Filmed Books and Plays, 1928-1967*. London: André Deutsch, 1968.

French, Brandon. *On the Verge of Revolt: Women in American Films of the Fifties*. New York: Frederick Ungar, 1978.

Gilbert, Sandra M., and Susan Gubar. *The Madwoman in the Attic: The Woman Writer and the Nineteenth-Century Literary Imagination*. New Haven, Conn.: Yale University Press, 1979.

Grimsted, David. *Melodrama Unveiled*. Chicago: University of Chicago Press, 1968.

Hagen, Ordean A. *Who Done It? A Guide to Detective, Mystery, and Suspense Fiction*. New York: R. R. Bowker, 1969.

Harper, Ralph. *The World of the Thriller*. Cleveland, Ohio: Case Western Reserve Press, 1969.

Haskell, Molly. *From Reverence to Rape: The Treatment of Women in the Movies*. New York: Holt, Rinehart and Winston, 1974.

Haycraft, Howard. *Murder for Pleasure*. New York: Appleton-Century, 1941.

_____, ed. *The Art of the Mystery Story*. New York: Simon and Schuster, 1946.

Hogarth, Basil. *Writing Thrillers for Profit: A Practical Guide*. London: A. & C. Black, 1936.

Kobal, John. *Romance and the Cinema*. London: Studio Vista, 1973.

Kowalski, Rosemary. *Women and Film*. Metuchen, N.J.: Scarecrow Press, 1976.

Lambert, Gavin. "The Making of *Gone With the Wind*," 2 parts, *Atlantic* 231 (February 1973): 37-51; and (March 1973): 56-72. Part II with comment on the movie by Andrew Sarris, Stanley Kauffman, Judith Crist, Arthur Schlesinger, Jr., and Richard Schickel.

McCreadie, Marcia, ed. *The American Movie Goddess*. New York: John Wiley, 1973.

Moers, Ellen. *Literary Women*. Garden City, N.Y.: Doubleday, 1977.

Murch, A. E. *The Development of the Detective Novel*. New York: Philosophical Library, 1958. Reprint. Port Washington, N.Y.: Kennikat, 1968.

Murder Manual: A Handbook for Mystery Story Writers. East San Diego, Calif.: Wight House Press, 1936.

Nye, Russel B. *The Unembarrassed Muse*. New York: Dial Press, 1970.

Parish, James Robert. *Hollywood's Great Love Teams*. New Rochelle, N.Y.: Arlington House, 1974.

_____. *The RKO Gals*. New Rochelle, N.Y.: Arlington House, 1974.

Perry, George. *Hitchcock*. Garden City, N.Y.: Doubleday, 1975.

Peterson, M. Jeanne. "The Victorian Governess: Status Incongruence in Family and Society." In *Suffer and Be Still: Women in the Victorian Age*, edited by Martha Vicinus. Bloomington, Ind.: Indiana University Press, 1972.

Pratley, Gerald. *The Cinema of David Lean*. New York: A. S. Barnes, 1974.

Pratt, William. *Scarlett Fever*. New York: Macmillan, 1977.

Rahill, Frank. *The World of Melodrama*. University Park, Pa.: Pennsylvania State University Press, 1967.

Rodell, Marie F. *Mystery Fiction: Theory and Technique*. New York: Duell, Sloan and Pearce, 1943.

Ruben, Renee. *"Jamaica Inn": The Story of the Film*. London: "The Mayflower" Pictures Corporation, Ltd., 1939.

Scott, Sutherland. *Blood in Their Ink: The March of the Modern Mystery Novel*. London: Stanley Paul, 1953.

Sennett, Ted. *Lunatics and Lovers: A Tribute to the Giddy and Glittering Era of the Screen's "Screwball" and Romantic Comedies*. New Rochelle, N.Y.: Arlington House, 1973.

Showalter, Elaine. *The Female Tradition in the English Novel: From Charlotte Brontë to Doris Lessing*. Princeton, N.J.: Princeton University Press, 1976.

Silver, Alain, and James Ursini. *David Lean and His Films*. London: Leslie Frewin, 1974.

Sklar, Robert. *Movie-Made America: A Social History of American Movies*. New York: Random House, 1975.

Spacks, Patricia Meyer. *The Female Imagination*. New York: Knopf, 1975.

Spoto, Donald. *The Art of Alfred Hitchcock: Fifty Years of His Motion Pictures*. New York: Hopkinson and Blake, 1976.

Thomson, H. Douglas. *Masters of Mystery*. 1931. Reprint. Folcroft, Pa.: Folcroft Press, 1969.

Thomson, Patricia. *The Victorian Heroine: A Changing Ideal*. London: Oxford University Press, 1956.

Wagner, Geoffrey. *The Novel and the Cinema*. Rutherford, N.J.: Fairleigh Dickinson University Press, 1975.

West, Katharine. *Chapter of Governesses: A Study of the Governess in English Fiction, 1800-1949*. London: Cohen and West, 1949.

Wood, Robin. *Hitchcock's Films*. 1966. Reprint, with "Retrospective." New York: A. S. Barnes, 1977.

Yacowar, Maurice. *Hitchcock's British Films*. Hamden, Conn.: Archon Books (The Shoe String Press), 1977.

PERIODICALS

The Writer. Boston: The Writer, Inc., 1887-.

CHAPTER *4*

Literary and Social History Approaches to Gothic and Romantic Fiction

Problems of definition in the field of gothic and romantic fiction are linked with those of approach. When the literary scholar refers to a novel as "romantic," that scholar is not using the term the way the popular culture scholar might. In the context of American fiction, Richard Chase suggested that all great American fiction could be called *romance*, to distinguish it from the more socially realistic fiction of Britain. That use of the word, however, does not adequately describe women's romances as a formula of popular fiction. In popular novels, the relationship between realism and romance is problematic, since the moral order of the world of popular romance is quite distinct from that in the romance of which Chase writes. John Cawelti draws the distinction by assigning to popular fiction the quality of "moral fantasy" in which, however realistic the surface details of the fiction may be, the moral order of the fictional world is fantastic, based upon idealizations of the way things should be. In addition to the problems of definition that plague the study of such fiction, however, there is also the larger issue of how to approach it. Literary historians have been understandably contemptuous of most such novels, thinking their time better spent studying more serious fiction, and refusing to grant aesthetic status to the books and their authors. Historians, even social historians, have often been more interested in mining the fiction for examples to illustrate their theses than in trying either to verify the novels' place in their own time or to understand the attraction of such fiction for its large audience of readers. Even recent feminist critics have sometimes based their conclusions upon their political predilections rather than upon more painstaking critical analysis. And, as with almost any subject that does not fit into an academic discipline as currently defined by universities and professional organizations, gothic and romantic fiction tends to fall between the cracks of scholarship. Some of the critical works discussed here are serious and enlightening. Many are antiquarian in nature; some are useful only as background to the subject.

Background material for understanding popular romantic fiction comprises a great number of works, but only a few merit citation. Most of the studies of the early romance, for example, are far too specialized to be applicable to American gothic and romantic fiction; the worlds of the two types of literature, however linked, are far apart. A notable exception, however, is a small volume by Gillian Beer, *The Romance*, a formalistic approach to the genre. Although it deals almost entirely with European and pre-1800 romances, its brief analysis of the audience for such narratives is suggestive for further study of women's romances. Beer notes that the romance allows readers a kind of "child-like" pleasure in that readers may enter its world at will. "It amplifies our experience: it does not press home upon us our immediate everyday concerns."[1] Discussing such important and serious precursors of modern gothic and romantic fiction as *Pamela* and *Northanger Abbey* Beer asserts: "The romances allowed their readers—who were mostly women—to immerse themselves without responsibility in a hectic world which made real life pale by comparison."[2] Her definition of the romance fits innumerable books by the authors discussed in this study. "We can think . . . of a cluster of properties: the themes of love and adventure, a certain withdrawal from their own societies on the part of both reader and romance hero, profuse sensuous detail, simplified characters (often with a suggestion of allegorical significance), a serene intermingling of the unexpected and the everyday, a complex and prolonged succession of incidents usually without a single climax, a happy ending, amplitude of proportions, a strongly enforced code of conduct to which all the characters must comply."[3]

Two monographs on English fiction are more directly applicable to American popular fiction. J. M. S. Tompkins's *The Popular Novel in England, 1770-1800* has a chapter on romantic and historical fiction that is exceptionally good for understanding the English backgrounds of the emerging American novel. An additional chapter on the gothic romance in England is similarly helpful. Robert Kiely's *The Romantic Novel in England* deals with aesthetic definitions of romantic fiction but does not make invidious comparisons between serious and popular fiction. Kiely's book does not discuss the popular audience for fiction since that is outside his subject, but he includes good chapters on *The Mysteries of Udolpho, The Monk, Northanger Abbey,* and *Wuthering Heights,* all serious books that must be considered important precursors of women's gothic and romantic novels. Two briefer essays also have good material on British literary backgrounds: Edith Birkhead's "Sentiment and Sensibility in the Eighteenth-Century Novel" and Patricia Meyer Spacks's "Ev'ry Woman is at Heart a Rake." The latter discusses women and sexuality in eighteenth-century British literature, suggesting motives and sources for women writers that may relate to those of American writers as well.

Dorothy Blakey's *The Minerva Press* is a study of one of the most successful British publishing houses issuing gothics, among other types of literature. There is no comparable study for American books until the mid-nineteenth century. An antiquarian work, Harry B. Weiss's *A Book About Chapbooks: The People's Literature of Bygone Times,* is a brief survey of the chapbook phenomenon. Many gothics appeared in chapbooks in England, and this book contains a list of American printers and publishers of chapbooks. A related study is William W. Watt's *Shilling Shockers of the Gothic School: A Study of Chapbook Gothic Romances,* although its subject matter is entirely British.

Because American gothic and romantic literature have been so derivative of British forms, the survey of images of women in literature, *Pamela's Daughters,* by Robert Palfrey Utter and Gwendolyn Bridges Needham, is exceptionally helpful for a work of literary history. Utter and Needham analyze women's economic and domestic roles, suggesting that the social position of women makes love stories particularly appealing in popular novels. They describe the typical plot of the English novel as having "love for the starting-post and marriage for the finish line."[4] Even an arranged and loveless marriage was often preferable to women's other alternatives: becoming a governess or paid companion, doing menial work and slipping out of the middle class, or prostitution. This book has only minimal discussion of American books and American heroines, but the superb analysis of literary types of women makes it essential for understanding the gothic and the romance in America.

There are two dated but basic surveys of the American novel that are useful, but neither is strong on critical analysis. Edward Wagenknecht's *Cavalcade of the American Novel* has an excellent bibliography, along with survey chapters on women novelists in the nineteenth century and on Mary Johnston. Arthur Hobson Quinn's *American Fiction: An Historical and Critical Survey* is, in essence, a collection of plot summaries.

It is more useful as a bibliographical tool. A third survey, Alexander Cowie's *The Rise of the American Novel*, is highly provocative in its conclusions about the American novel, especially the American gothic novel. Cowie argues, for example, that America never developed a gothic tradition like that of England; for there were none of the important elements available in American society out of which writers could produce such fiction. There was not enough convention, little tradition, and no acknowledged social hierarchy in American society. On the other hand, when American authors tried to write gothic fiction, the best of them were able to use Indians and the vast West as substitutes for Gothic castles and terrors. Cowie also has fine individual sections on a wide variety of romantic novels. Even more provocative is Leslie A. Fiedler's *Love and Death in the American Novel*. Fiedler's definition of gothic and romantic is probably too narrow; but his evaluation of the gothic in which he draws connections between death and the orgasm, suggesting that the approach of danger in the gothic represents a strong sexual urge toward death, is very suggestive. Since in most gothic fiction, the culmination of the love story and the salvation from danger are simultaneous and linked, his argument seems relevant. He also defines as clearly as anyone the types of women characters found in early American novels. These types of women still abound in popular gothic and romantic novels.

Mary Sumner Benson's *Women in Eighteenth-Century America* has a very good chapter, "Women in Early American Literature," with a fine survey of novels, plays, and magazines as they related to American women, although she consciously ignores "numerous second-rate novels of romantic adventure." Two essential references on American fiction prior to 1830, one very old but still useful, one relatively recent, should also be consulted. Lily D. Loshe's *The Early American Novel, 1789-1830* was first published in 1907. She defines the forms of the first fiction in America. More thorough and analytical is Henri Petter's *The Early American Novel*. Petter is a German scholar whose analysis of American forms of fiction includes American uses of gothic conventions, in his chapter on "Mystery and Terror," and a long and excellent section on "the love story," in which he discriminates between types and conventions. Petter also writes informatively about the general attack on novel reading during this period, which often was an attack on women's novels in general and the gothic in particular. Most of the attack was against novels as a "waste of time" and "not true," although the supposed pernicious influence of such fiction on suggestible young female minds also came in for its share of criticism. The book is extensively annotated and has a number of bibliographical aids.

Another analysis of the attack on fiction is G. H. Orians's "Censure of Fiction in American Magazines and Romances, 1789-1810," a study of the outcry about fiction. There is also a fascinating, brief article on a very odd and obscure book, *A Female Marine* (1814) by Lucy Brewer. Alexander Medlicott, Jr., in "The Legend of Lucy Brewer: An Early American Novel," describes an adventurous tale of a woman warrior who served as a rifleman on the U.S.S. *Constitution*. Although Lucy was apparently an active heroine, in the way that no others were until the Western heroines of dime novels later in the century, she marries and settles down at the end of the book.

Surveys of American popular culture or popular fiction mention gothic and romantic fiction, although they rarely give them full-scale treatment. The best of these is Russel B. Nye's *The Unembarrased Muse*, the standard history of American popular arts. Nye describes a number of formulas and authors whose works lie within the boundaries of the gothic and the romance. Nye is much more interested in description than in castigating popular fiction for low quality, so the book is marked by a liberality of spirit and data that is refreshing and helpful to the scholar. Frank Luther Mott's *Golden Multitudes* is a study of the bestseller in America. It is out of date and devoted to trivia, making it more useful for reference than for analysis. Mott's perspective on the bestseller, however, sometimes leads to more problems than it solves, so users of this book should be cautious and skeptical. Mott's interest is in number of copies of each work sold, and he relies upon estimates from date of publication to the present. The result is that some books are identified as bestsellers in this volume that were never popular in their own day, but they have reached Mott's list because of their steady sales over a period of time. Consequently, Mott's work is not strictly a study of popular culture, although within its limitations it can be valuable. Much more analytically and conceptually valid is James D. Hart's *The Popular Book: A History of America's Literary Taste*. Hart's book, as the title indicates, centers on the issue of varying taste in different periods. There are many references to gothic and romantic fiction throughout the book. Carl Bode's *Anatomy of American Popular Culture, 1840-1861* analyzes romantic fiction, among other popular entertainment forms. Mary Noel's *Villains Galore: The Heyday of the Popular Story Weekly* is a superficial, but still useful, survey of stories in weekly story papers. She is good for description of plot, but there is no bibliography and no system of analysis.

The major theoretical work of popular culture scholarship is John G. Cawelti's *Adventure, Mystery, and Romance*. Cawelti is exceptionally insightful on the definition of popular romance and particularly suggestive on the relationship between the romance and what he calls the social melodrama. "The crucial defining characteristic of romance," he writes, "is not that it stars a female but that its organizing action is the development of a love relationship, usually between a man and a woman. . . . Romances often contain elements of adventure, but the dangers function as a means of challenging and cementing the love relationship."[5] Scholars will be working with and extending Cawelti's formulaic approach to popular fiction for some time; this book can be ignored only at one's peril. Another book that approaches the popular novel in the nineteenth century in an interesting way is Henry Nash Smith's *Democracy and the Novel*. Smith, who pioneered the use of popular fiction in the analysis of cultural myths in *Virgin Land*, is concerned in this book about nineteenth-century authors and the popular audience. He discusses such serious writers as Hawthorne, Melville, Howells, and Twain, as well as the unique publishing phenomenon, *Norwood* by Henry Ward Beecher. A related essay by Smith is "The Scribbling Women and the Cosmic Success Story." Kathryn Weibel's *Mirror, Mirror: Images of Women Reflected in Popular Culture* is an important popular culture approach that surveys women's images by medium: fiction, television, movies, magazines and advertising, and clothes. Norman Cantor and Michael Wertham's *History of Popular Culture* is a collection of excerpts of material on popular culture from the ancient Greeks to the hippies. A relevant section of that book is David Daiches's "The Novel As a Reflection of Middle-Class Attitudes," in which he discusses the effects on the English novel of middle-class attitudes toward marriage, the family, and society. Bruno Bettelheim's *The Uses of Enchantment*, a psychological study of fairy tales, offers particularly useful rereadings of several of the most familiar tales, such as Snow White and Cinderella. Because the plots of women's romances often resemble those of fairy tales, this is a literary approach that should prove helpful. Also useful is an essay by Marcia R. Lieberman, " 'Some Day My Prince Will Come': Female Acculturation Through the Fairy Tale," a study of the stories in the *Blue Fairy Book* (1934) in terms of what they show young girls to expect about their future.

Since most of the critical work available on the gothic novel deals with the eighteenth century and with British versions, most of it is of use in the study of American popular gothics only as background. If American authors are considered in these studies, they are authors such as Poe and Hawthorne, not the popular authors whose indebtedness to earlier gothic forms was different from theirs. Much critical work tries to provide definitions of the gothic and of its various subgenres, although Mary McCarthy, speaking in Amsterdam in 1973, argued that there is no such thing as gothic literature, in her speech, "Can There Be a Gothic Literature?" She suggests that the range of items that are called *gothic*, from architecture to literature, from medieval artists to Iris Murdoch, is too great for one definition to cover. One is tempted to agree after reading many of the attempts to provide structure over such a diffuse topic.

The chapter "Literary Influences" in Kenneth Clark's *The Gothic Revival: An Essay in the History of Taste* links the Graveyard Poets and the gothic novelists with the gothic revival in architecture in England. Three specialized studies of the gothic novel in England are Eino Railo's *The Haunted Castle*, Montague Summers's *The Gothic Quest*, and Devendra P. Varma's *The Gothic Flame*. Railo is especially good in his descriptions of the various strains of the gothic in England. Summers is far too much the ideologue and bibliophile for the book to be of critical use; he is interested in "spreading the faith" rather than in analysis. Varma, on the other hand, provides a lucid discussion of the gothic novel in England, and is particularly helpful in his analysis of the various ways in which gothic fiction became diffused through other forms of literature after its heyday. An appendix analyzes the influence of the gothic on the detective novel, and the bibliography is extensive. Another study, *The Gothic Romance* by Hans Moebius, published in Leipzig in 1902, seems to be available only in German.

Edith Birkhead's *The Tale of Terror* is excellent on the supernatural in English gothic fiction, but traces the gothic in America only through Charles Brockden Brown, Poe, Hawthorne, and Irving; she is more interested in the influence of the gothic on serious literature than in its influence on popular culture. Michael Sadleir's " 'All Horrid?': Jane Austen and the Gothic Romance" in *Things Past* is a fascinating essay describing the specific gothic novels Austen satirized in *Northanger Abbey*. Since Austen was influential on authors of women's literature, this essay should be consulted. Also interesting is "Night Thoughts on the Gothic Novel," by Lowry Nelson, Jr., especially for its suggestive discussion of the gothic hero/villain. Male figures in modern gothic novels are only rarely as complex and ambivalent as those in the early British gothic, but the modern writers, especially, seem to use the same characteristics and split them between hero and villain. Of little use in the discussion of popular gothic is Robert D. Hume and Robert L. Platzner's exchange on the gothic in *PMLA*. Much more to the point than any of the above, for purpose of analysis of popular novels, is a quasi-serious, brief article by Clell T. Peterson, "Spotting the Gothic Novel," in *Graduate Student of English*. Peterson list sixteen characteristics of the gothic novel, most of which are applicable to modern gothics as well as to earlier versions.

Oral Sumner Coad's "The Gothic Element in American Literature Before 1835" is an influential analytical survey; George L. Phillips's "The Gothic Element in the American Novel Before 1830" is similarly useful. O. W. Long's "Werther in America" traces the influences of Goethe on American fiction, while Jane Lundblad's *Nathaniel Hawthorne and the Tradition of the Gothic Romance* shows how Hawthorne adapted gothic elements in his own work. Neither is especially relevant to the study of popular fiction, although both should be consulted for definitions of the gothic. Lundblad's work, however, taken together with Michael Davitt Bell's more theoretical study, *Hawthorne and the Historical Romance of New England*, shows how popular traditions in fiction influence the work of serious writers.

Of specific value in examining early American gothic fiction is Sister Mary Mauritia Redden's *The Gothic Fiction in the American Magazines, 1765-1800*, a dissertation published in 1939. Redden includes definitions of the characteristics of both British and American gothic fiction and plot summaries of many gothic stories in American magazines. She says that the gothic first appeared in American magazines in 1785; almost all of the stories in this period were anonymous imitations of Mrs. Ann Radcliffe's works. The appendixes include magazine lists, a bibliography, and a chronological listing of stories.

Sometimes introductions to collections and reprints of gothic fiction can be excellent sources of criticism. Especially noteworthy are two introductions to reprinted novels in the Arno Press series, *Gothic Novels*, edited by Devendra P. Varma. Robert D. Hume's introduction to *Longsword* contains a long history of eighteenth-century fiction and the place of the gothic within it. Robert D. Mayo's introduction to *Grasville Abbey* is a history of the popular gothic novel in the 1790s. A quick but unanalytical summary of the gothic is Robert Donald Spector's introduction to his edition of *Seven Masterpieces of Gothic Horror*. None of the selections in that volume is representative of American popular literature. A similar collection, *Gothic Tales of Terror*, is edited by Peter Haining. More useful than either of these, however, is another collection, edited by G. Richard Thompson. The Thompson volume, *Romantic Gothic Tales, 1790-1840*, includes a fine collection of serious short stories influenced by the gothic, but its main significance is in the introduction by Thompson in which he skillfully distinguishes between what he calls "high" and "low" gothic, the former characterized by *dread* and the latter by *fear*.[6] Dividing the gothic into four modes—

historical, explained, supernatural, and ambiguous—Thompson succinctly summarizes decades of scholarship in a short piece and offers his own lucid evaluation of the place of the gothic in the context of romantic fiction. Thompson draws from, even if he partially disagrees with, the recent work of Ellen Moers in *Literary Women*, especially her analysis of the "female gothic" to be discussed below in the context of feminist scholarship. Thompson's division of "high" and "low" modes seems justified; it should be noted that this study deals almost entirely with works Thompson would characterize as being in the "low" mode. The introduction also includes an excellent bibliography, although it is unannotated. Two unpublished Ph.D. dissertations deal specifically with relevant issues: Raymond Winfield Mise's "The Gothic Heroine and the Nature of the Gothic Novel" and Marietta R. Ranieri's "The Self Behind the Self: The Americanization of the Gothic." Two popularized anthologies of short stories by women authors are useless critically, but they contain interesting obscure examples of gothic and romantic stories along with occasional biographical data. *Ladies of the Gothic: Tales of Romance and Terror Told by The Gentle Sex* includes works by Emily Brontë, Ann Radcliffe, Jane Austen, Mary Shelley, and Harriet Prescott Spofford. *Mistresses of Mystery: Two Centuries of Suspense Stories by the Gentle Sex* includes work by Harriet Prescott Spofford. Both are edited by Seon Manley and Gogo Lewis, who have coedited several volumes of stories on similar themes.

General literary studies sometimes have sections discussing the influence of the gothic on later literature. For the most part, the emphasis is upon serious works of fiction rather than popular, but some of the studies can be useful. Stanley Bank edited a collection entitled *American Romanticism: A Shape for Fiction* in which he published selections from the writings on the writing of Charles Brockden Brown, Cooper, Poe, Hawthorne, Melville, Simms, and Irving. Each of these authors was influenced by the popular gothic traditions of his day, and Bank's interesting introduction traces the authors' use of gothic and romantic conventions. Masao Miyoshi's *The Divided Self: A Perspective on the Literature of the Victorians* suggests that the convention of the divided self in English Victorian literature can be traced from the gothic to the Byronic hero and beyond. This theoretical discussion is exceptionally important in understanding the emotional and intellectual appeal of the gothic. Irving Malin's *New American Gothic* discusses the influence of the gothic on modern American writers. Newton Arvin's "Melville and the Gothic Novel" traces Melville's knowledge of gothic fiction, especially the novels of Ann Radcliffe, showing how the use of gothic trappings and symbols was adapted by Melville, most notably in

Pierre. Gary R. Thompson's *The Gothic Imagination: Essays in Dark Romanticism* is a collection of essays by scholars reevaluating the gothic through Kafka. Most of them argue that the gothic is Quest literature, a search for the ideal. Although the book is entirely concerned with serious British literature, the argument that the gothic represents a quest for the ideal illuminates its adaptability for women authors and readers. In most gothic novels for women, the heroine must go through a series of hazards and terrors before she finds what she is looking for, a perfect mate. As in Quest literature, she must earn her reward by suffering and by performing well under pressure. By placing this kind of fictional pattern in the consciousness of a woman, authors can easily adapt it to the search for a husband that is the basic topic of both gothic and romantic fiction for women. Margot Northey's *The Haunted Wilderness: The Gothic and the Grotesque in Canadian Fiction* is also relevant and useful. Northey offers an excellent analysis of some Canadian gothic works and shows that the gothic in America and Canada developed in similar ways outside of the European tradition. Especially interesting is her analysis of Ann Hebert's *Kamouraska* (1970), a fine gothic novel with dark undertones that is most familiar to Americans as the source of a film adaptation starring Genevieve Bujold several years ago. Northey also perceptively suggests the close relationship between gothic and sentimental romances.

> Although all romance strikes an emotional chord, it makes a difference whether the chord is in a minor or a major key. Compared to the gothic novel, with its frightening mood of mystery or estrangement, the sentimental romance has an atmosphere of optimism rather than doom, with a final reassurance of conventional sentiments and attitudes. As Leslie Fiedler has illustrated, when the gothic romance raises the spectre of inscrutable evil, often exemplified by incest and other unnatural relationships, the sentimental romance presents the ideal of chaste love and virtue triumphant. . . . Yet since both types spring basically from the same imaginative fount, it is not surprising that gothic elements are repeatedly found in the sentimental romance and vice versa.[7]

Studies of the fiction in women's magazines often provide material on the romantic elements of such fiction, although there are few of these that approach the subject from a literary perspective. A recent book that provides important basic information about love stories in women's magazines is Mirabel Cecil's *Heroines in Love, 1750-1974*. Cecil surveys magazine romantic fiction over more than two centuries, providing in each chapter a breezy overview of a particular era as well as an excerpt or a representative story from a magazine. She covers both British and American fiction. The work is comprehensive, but contains no bibliography or analysis. It is more suggestive than useful, but is essential nonetheless since these stories are so rarely surveyed elsewhere. Another study of magazines, much narrower and more scholarly, is Ellen Hoekstra's "The Pedestal Myth Reinforced: Women's Magazine Fiction, 1900-1920" in Russel B. Nye's *New Dimensions in Popular Culture*.

Before the feminist movement in scholarship, several studies of women's popular fiction were published. Some of these were proto-feminist; others were condescending; still others were evenhanded. Many of them are still relevant, and the best of these is Herbert Ross Brown's *The Sentimental Novel in America, 1789-1860*, published in 1940 and only partially superseded in 1978 by Nina Baym's study, *Woman's Fiction*, to be discussed below. Brown used the catalog of a New York circulating library to identify books from the period, and he wrote a delightful and solid book on the types of fiction that were the most popular. Much analysis of romantic fiction is included; especially interesting is Brown's analysis of the seduction story. Helen W. Papashvily's *All the Happy Endings* is a more popularized book; it is a protofeminist approach to the domestic romance, arguing that the books are actually submerged revolts against the male-dominated culture, an argument made later and more systematically by Nina Baym. Papashvily has a good, but unannotated, bibliography of secondary sources prior to 1954, but no list of primary sources. Her chatty, biographical approach to the material is especially useful on E. D. E. N. Southworth. Alexander Cowie's "The Vogue of the Domestic Novel" is an excerpt from his larger study. Fred L. Pattee's *The Feminine Fifties* has a survey chapter on the "scribbling women," but the book is marred by its lack of bibliography and its condescending attitude. Beatrice Hofstadter's "Popular Culture and the Romantic Heroine" is an analysis of six popular novels from the mid-nineteenth century to the mid-twentieth. It is a good and interesting comparative study of how changing types of women affect images in women's romances. Much more diffuse, although worth noting, is Robert J. Ward's "Europe in American Historical Romances, 1890-1910." An overview of the characters and settings of 118 novels by Americans, the article is cursory but provides material for further analysis.

Three other studies of women in fiction that were published before the women's studies movement are also helpful. Dorothy Yost Deegan's *The Stereotype of the Single Woman in American Novels* uses lists of significant American books, analyzing them for stereotypes. It suggests that women's roles in fiction are much more limited than in life and that American women should be prepared for the possibility of living the single life. William Wassertrom's *Heiress of All the Ages: Sex and Sentiment in the Genteel Tradition* argues that in genteel fiction from the 1830s to World War I the function of sex was domesticated in marriage, reconciling the figures of the virgin and the mistress in that of the wife. Wassertrom refers almost entirely to serious fiction, but his analysis also bears on popular romances. Essentially a survey, Gerarda Maria Kooiman-von Middendorp's *The Hero in the Feminine Novel* contains chapters on Ann Radcliffe, Austen, and the Brontës, among others. Each of these should be read with the Utter and Needham study, *Pamela's Daughters.*

From the 1820s through most of the nineteenth century, popular fiction, especially gothic and romantic types, was dominated by a large group of women writers, referred to by Hawthorne and others as the "scribbling women." Some of these novels were historical, a common convention in gothic fiction, and many of those in the early part of the century were set in colonial New England. Some of these books, for example, Catharine Maria Sedgwick's *Hope Leslie* (1827) and Eliza B. Lee's *Naomi* (1848), seem to bridge the gothic and the romance using the American landscape, Indians, and the wilderness to offer adventure (as suggested by Cowie) but with heroines who finally win their true loves through steadfast behavior. Michael Davitt Bell's *Hawthorne and the Historical Romance of New England* sees Hawthorne in the context of other writers, many of them women, who wrote between 1820 and 1850 about Puritan New England. He suggests that Hawthorne's works are related to this fictional tradition, and he sees a significance in the use of a woman as a rebel whose rebellion is often focussed upon marriage, but whose problems can always be solved through marriage. This is the central paradox of much modern gothic writing as well. Bell shows a broader significance to the love plot by suggesting that the Puritan fathers perform the function of impediment to the marriage and must be vanquished, thus reaffirming the nineteenth century's assumptions about their Puritan forbears. An essay by Bell, "History and Romance Convention in Catharine Sedgwick's *Hope Leslie*," is a thorough analysis of how the romantic plot in that novel weaves in and around the other elements and provides a moral center for the narrative. Both Nina Baym and Ann Douglas have also commented upon the significance of this conventional Puritan historical narrative in romantic fiction.

Other studies, relatively uninfluenced by the critical and theoretical debates of the women's movement, are also helpful. Bertha-Monica Stearns published two short essays, "Before Godey's" and "Early New

England Magazines for Ladies." Both are surveys, the first of approximately one hundred magazines catering to women in America before the success of *Godey's Lady's Book* and the other a survey of later magazines with a heavy concentration upon Sarah Josepha Hale, editor of *Godey's*. Joseph Satterthwaite's "The Tremulous Formula: Form and Technique in *Godey's* Fiction" suggests that the magazine's fiction was "the epitome of the sentimental spirit" and was mostly sad in tone. H. Smith's "Feminism and the Household Novel" describes the motives for writing of some mid-nineteenth century women authors. Leslie Smith's "Through Rose-Colored Glasses: Some American Victorian Sentimental Novels" is a good basic study of Mary Jane Holmes, E. D. E. N. Southworth, and Sylvanus Cobb, Jr. Two other basic introductory surveys are Donald A. Koch's introduction to his edition of Holmes's *Tempest and Sunshine* and Maria Susanna Cummins's *The Lamplighter*, and Robert Bogard's "Amelia Barr, Augusta Evans Wilson, and the Sentimental Novel." John T. Frederick's article, "Hawthorne's 'Scribbling Women,' " evaluates Hawthorne's antipathy to such fiction by showing its competition to serious writers.

In the past decade, and especially in the last four years, the influence of women's studies in scholarship has become apparent in approaches to romantic and gothic fiction. The studies range from the blindly political to the brilliantly innovative, and the number of new essays and monographs seems to increase geometrically each year. An early feminist anthology of material on women in popular culture contains some good, although uneven, work. *Images of Women in Fiction: Feminist Perspectives*, edited by Susan Koppelman Cornillon, appeared in 1972. Although many of the articles are relevant and worth consulting, two are especially useful. The most interesting is a suggestive, if superficial, essay by Joanna Russ, "What Can a Heroine Do? or, Why Women Can't Write." Russ argues that the useful myths of culture that inform literary works are male myths and that women exist in them only as reflected entities; thus the central experience for women in fiction is courtship and marriage. The rest of women's lives cannot be easily portrayed in fiction because the culture has not allowed women's full lives to reach conventional status in literary works. The other interesting essay is "Popular Literature as Social Reinforcement: The Case of *Charlotte Temple*" by Kathleen Conway McGrath.

A growing list of works by women scholars, primarily nineteenth-century historians interested in New England, has added greatly to knowledge of romantic fiction between 1820 and 1870. Some of these studies are not directly about popular fiction, but they all approach women in American culture in ways that illuminate the fiction and

its background; and many of them use the fiction as evidence in the
study. The beneficiary of a growing belief that American women's
lives and culture have been slighted in conventional literary and historical
scholarship, most of these studies have the explicit purpose of recovering
lost data and redefining priorities for scholarship. There are, of course,
serious methodological and conceptual problems in such work, and some of
these authors confront those issues more directly than do others. The task of
re-creating lives and drawing information from incomplete and submerged
material is one important problem that most of them have handled effectively. However, the larger issue of generalizing from fiction to life is more
problematic in some of these works. That issue will be discussed in Chapter
5 of this study, but should be noted here as a basic problem in much of the
new research.

Barbara Welter was a pioneer in women's studies scholarship on
the nineteenth century; her *American Quarterly* article, "The Cult of
True Womanhood," has become a classic and is widely quoted and
cited. Welter argues that the culture of the nineteenth century exalted
an idea of womanhood that canonized the virtues of "purity, piety,
domesticity, and submissiveness," and she cites ample data to support
her contention. This essay and others by Welter are reprinted in her
Dimity Convictions: The American Woman in the Nineteenth Century, a
volume that also contains essays on adolescence, medical problems of
women, anti-intellectualism, women's religious novels, the detective
writer Anna Katharine Green, and the feminist critic Margaret Fuller.
In her introduction to a collection of writings by American women,
The Oven Birds: American Women on Womanhood, 1820-1920, Gail Thain
Parker discusses the problems of women who lacked heroinic models
and how this affected their writing. Kathryn Kish Sklar's excellent
biography, *Catharine Beecher: A Study in American Domesticity*, adds
much to an understanding of the woman as writer in this period;
although Beecher did not write novels, and her sister Harriet Beecher
Stowe was much more than a women's writer, many romantic novelists
of the period, like Beecher, wrote advice books for women on
etiquette, domestic economy, and education. This biography of a single
woman who wrote for women is an important source of information
on the conditions for women writers in that period. A more general
study, and another excellent one, is Susan P. Conrad's *Perish the Thought:
Intellectual Women in Romantic America, 1830-1860*. Conrad argues that
the work of the popular novelists, with its emphasis upon home and
love and marriage, reinforced the problems of female intellectuals in
America. Nancy F. Cott's *The Bonds of Womanhood: "Woman's Sphere"
in New England, 1780-1835* is a survey of diaries, journals, and letters

by ordinary, unknown New England women. Cott tries to define the conditions of women's lives and the changes in those conditions during the period. The book is excellent background, even though Cott deals very little with fiction. However, the women she writes about might well have formed a part of the audience for gothic and romantic fiction. Another important feminist study is Carroll Smith-Rosenberg's "The Female World of Love and Ritual: Relations Between Women in Nineteenth-Century America" in *Signs*, the journal in which much of the most significant women's studies scholarship has been published in recent years.

Feminist scholarship on Victorian women in England is also helpful in defining women's roles and images in the nineteenth century. Among the most useful and accessible collections are two edited by Martha Vicinus. The first, *Suffer and Be Still*, includes most notably a fine essay by M. Jeanne Peterson, "The Victorian Governess: Status Incongruence in Family and Society." The second Vicinus volume, *A Widening Sphere: Changing Roles of Victorian Women*, contains a good study by Sally Mitchell, "The Forgotten Women of the Period: Penny Weekly Family Magazines of the 1840s and 1850s," along with an excellent introduction by Vicinus in which she delineates the relationship between women's literature and women's lives in Victorian England. She argues that literature rarely encompassed all of women's problems but that, in its concentration upon love and marriage, it shaped women's perceptions of themselves and their society. Sally Mitchell is also the author of another essay, "Sentiment and Suffering: Women's Recreational Reading in the 1860s." Two additional studies of British society are excellent for the social context of popular literature for women. Patricia R. Thomson's *The Victorian Heroine, A Changing Ideal* has a long, fine section on the governess as a fictional convention. Leonore Davidoff's *The Best Circles: Society, Etiquette, and the Season* is a social history of British Society, the setting for innumerable gothic and romantic novels in both centuries. Davidoff's analysis of how Society controlled women's lives illuminates the patterns and assumptions of women's fiction.

A collection of essays from the 1973 Berkshire Conference on Women, Mary Hartman and Lois W. Banner's *Clio's Consciousness Raised*, contains no work directly on fiction but several fine studies on the history of women's medical problems and sexuality. Another feminist essay that is useful is Glenda Gates Riley's "The Subtle Subversion: Changes in the Traditional Images of the American Woman."

Recent feminist literary studies have also flourished and sparked controversy. In addition to the studies of serious writers in the nineteenth century, discussed in the previous chapter (Showalter, Spacks, Moers, and Gilbert and Gubar), a researcher might consult Judith Fetterley's *The Resisting Reader: A Feminist Approach to American Fiction,* Elizabeth Hardwick's *Seduction and Betrayal: Women and Literature,* and Mary Ellmann's *Thinking About Women.* In 1978, two different and vitally important works of feminist scholarship were published; taken together, they delineate some of the main problems and controversies of feminist approaches to women's popular fiction. Ann Douglas's *The Feminization of American Culture* has received more critical attention and controversial commentary than has Nina Baym's *Woman's Fiction: A Guide to Novels By and About Women in America, 1820-1870.* Baym and Douglas acknowledge each other's work and "agree to disagree." Douglas suggests that there was a progressive loss of power for both women and the clergy in the nineteenth century; the result was a pervasive and evasive sentimentality. The book provides excellent background for women's romantic fiction. Deploring the debased sentimentalism of the period, she argues that it tended to submerge and pacify the powerless rather than invigorate them. In 1980, writing about recent films and the Harlequin Romances in *New Republic,* Douglas extended her argument, saying that Harlequins are a kind of soft-core pornography for women and that they implicate women in their own subjection while mounting an attack on the liberated woman. In two scholarly pieces prior to her book's publication, Douglas, writing as Ann D. Wood, discussed other women writers. "The 'Scribbling Women' and Fanny Fern: Why Women Wrote" is a discussion of motives and how women writers tried to avoid being threatening to men, although Fanny Fern rejected that stance and expressed more direct hostility. In "Mrs. Sigourney and the Sensibility of Inner Space," she evaluated Mrs. Sigourney's poems, suggesting how the poet created an acceptable public persona through her poetry that served certain psychic functions in her unhappy private life.

On the other hand, Baym's book is based upon a close and critical reading of the texts of a large number of women's novels. She provides long plot descriptions and analyses for many of these forgotten books, and builds upon available biographical and critical feminist scholarship. Although Baym's book is highly significant, especially in what it adds to earlier analyses such as those of Brown and Papashvily, she occasionally strains her thesis by trying to make too much of the supposed "feminism" of the authors with whom she deals. Baym, for example, argues that "her" authors are more significant than those who write "gothics" and thus fails to see the clear connections between them. She suggests that the books she analyzes, in contrast to the more formulaic novels, deal with the development of women's ability and self-esteem, providing models for independent action for women readers. The books do, in fact, often focus upon women developing a sense of self and the ability to function in the world, but almost invariably those developments lead to marriage. Even in Sedgwick's *Married or Single?* (1857), the woman who contemplates the single life marries in the end. In addition, the development of the self in women is also a theme of much gothic fiction. In making the argument that women's novels in the nineteenth century are the carriers of a covert revolt, both Baym and Papashvily seem to assume that a fictional revolt is analogous to a real one. As Chapter 5 will show, the relationship between reader and novel is a complex one, and one cannot assume that reader identification with an unconventional woman suggests that the reader, too, is unconventional. To the contrary, one might just as easily suggest that such an identification is merely a defusing of uncomfortable tensions in real life and that women may resort to fiction as an alternative to psychosis or illness in handling those tensions. At any event, the pervasiveness of marriage as the culmination of these books seems to argue against their genuine unconventionality. The problem, however, is a serious one conceptually, and Douglas and Baym, representing opposite views from a basically feminist perspective, have defined it, although neither has the last word.

Other authors have also approached the issue. Mary Ryan's unpublished dissertation, "American Society and the Cult of Domesticity," is cited by Baym as supporting her contention that the novels are supposed to be orthodox but are unconsciously rebellious. Mary Kelley's fine "The Sentimentalists: Promise and Betrayal in the Home" is a more balanced view. Kelley argues that in the fiction of the sentimentalists, their overt intentions and their covert results are often at war. Her view is that women writers were neither so revolutionary and angry as portrayed by Baym, Papashvily, and others, nor so busy pacifying themselves and denying their real needs as Welter and Douglas might seem to suggest. An evaluation of the issue in more modern women's fiction is found in Kay J. Mussell's unpublished dissertation, "The World of Modern Gothic Fiction: American Women and Their Social Myths," centering on the work of Mary Stewart, Victoria Holt, Phyllis Whitney, and Dorothy Eden. The same authors are the subject of Mussell's "Beautiful and Damned: The Sexual Woman in Modern Gothic Fiction."

A provocative essay, "On Reading Trash" by Lillian S. Robinson, is an evaluation of women's literature by a scholar who has found pleasure in reading much of what other scholars have disdained. Robinson discusses in an autobiographical mode such types of literature as the gothic, the historical, the Regency or historical romances, and the straight romances. The bulk of her essay is an extended comparison between Jane Austen and Georgette Heyer that avoids qualitative aesthetic judgments in favor of an approach that concentrates upon the "pleasure-giving" aspects of each.

In addition to literary criticism and social history, there is one additional area of literary history that can be helpful to researchers in looking at women's gothic and romantic novels. Since such fiction has been so pervasive in popular reading for two centuries, studies of publishing in America often include information about it. These studies are especially valuable because they usually try to avoid pejorative judgments. Historians of publishing and publishing houses are interested in books as a commercial commodity, not in making literary or historical judgments about merit. *Publishers Weekly* is, of course, a similar source, since its primary audience—booksellers, reviewers, publishing industry personnel—want to know what is going on in the industry rather than what a critic thinks of a book. Many publishing histories are dated and antiquarian in tone, but some are very useful.

John Williams Tebbel's *A History of Book Publishing in the United States* is a three-volume reference work that is invaluable. It includes information on publishers, bestsellers, and copyright laws, and it is fairly up to date. A useful survey is Charles A. Madison's *Book Publishing in America*, organized by publisher. Using this book, it is relatively easy to see at a glance what sorts of fiction different publishing houses have specialized in during various periods of literary history. Published in 1966, the book covers American history from the colonial era to modern times. Somewhat older than the Madison book is H. Lehman-Haupt, L. C. Wroth, and Rollo Silver's *The Book in America*, a general reference history of the book that is especially good on the background to book publishing.

Some specialized works can also be helpful. Although it does not mention gothic and romantic fiction as such, a general discussion of publication of inexpensive books in America can be found in C. Hugh Holman's "Cheap Books and the Public Interest: Paperbound Book Publishing in Two Centuries," published in *Frontiers of American Culture*. A published master's thesis in library science in 1937 also studies the production of inexpensive books in America. Raymond H. Shove's *Cheap Book Production in the United States, 1870-1891* is valuable because of its thoroughness for the years it covers and also because of Shove's essential discussion of the impact of copyright law changes on American book publishing and authors. Shove offers a year-by-year summary, economical and statistical, of what was being published during the period, as well as discussions of the publishers themselves. He also outlines the effect of the International Copyright Law of 1891 on a book industry where pirating and reprints without compensation had been common. The International Copyright Law was especially important in America, since up to that point, American publishers were economically wise to print British books rather than American ones because they did not have to pay royalties to British authors. British authors, of course, complained about the practice, but American authors suffered no less since it was more difficult for them to place a book with a publisher who could make more money without paying an author.

Occasionally, a specialized study done for an industry or professional group will also be helpful. For example, a study done by William Miller for the American Library Association in 1949, *The Book Industry*, offers a good overview of the contemporary situation, including data on publishing houses, book clubs, sales of books, editorial policies, and other related issues. Even more valuable is an impressive recent survey done by the firm of Yankelovich, Skelly, and White for the Book Industry Study Group. Entitled *Consumer Research Study on Reading and Book Purchasing*, the report holds a wealth of information for scholars. Gothic and romantic fiction are included as categories in the survey. This study, and other similar ones that concentrate on readers rather than on books, will be discussed more fully in Chapter 5.

Four other volumes of publishing history could also be consulted. Eugene Exman's *The Brothers Harper* is a simple study of the founders of the Harper's publishing enterprise. Quentin Reynolds's *The Fiction Factory* is a readable history of the firm of Street and Smith, publishers of dime novels. William Charvat's *Literary Publishing in America, 1790-1850* is a slim volume of three essays with invaluable background on the economics and distribution of books in that period. Charvat says he is setting out to study "that middle brow, middle range of literature, serious but not necessarily original, which is, and always has been, the bread and butter of respectable publishers."[8] Esther J. Carrier's *Fiction in Public Libraries, 1876-1900* is a solid, but mundane, compendium of information on what public libraries were providing their patrons. The most interesting section for the study of gothic and romantic fiction is the discussion of E. D. E. N. Southworth, Mary Jane Holmes, Caroline Hentz, and some of their contemporaries in terms of the censorship controversies of the times. Much criticism of the value of such novels was current in the late Victorian era, and this book sheds light on those critiques. Another approach to the same controversies, and a more scholarly one, is Dee Garrison's *American Quarterly* article, "Immoral Fiction in the Late Victorian Library." Based on a study of an 1881 questionnaire by the American Library Association to seventy major public libraries, Garrison's essay cites a number of authors whose works were controversial, including Ann Sophia Stephens, Mrs. Southworth, Mary Jane Holmes, Caroline Lee Hentz, and Augusta Jane Wilson. Like Baym, Garrison asserts that these authors spoke for an unconventional notion of womanhood and became controversial in the context of the feminist controversies and the rapidly changing roles of women.

Clearly, there is ample room for future scholars to build upon the work described in this chapter in order to better understand the place of women's romantic fiction in the culture of American women readers. Although many of these studies are distinguished, many others are pedestrian, simplistic, and ideological. Little is gained by applying literary standards of excellence and merit to women's popular romances, and the novels are not well served by revisionist theories that overemphasize their radical qualities. The next chapter will suggest a strategy for placing these works in their own context and of unraveling some of the complex tangles in their interpretation.

NOTES

1. Gillian Beer, *The Romance* (London: Methuen, 1970), p. 9.

2. Ibid., p. 53.

3. ibid., p. 10.

4. Robert Palfrey Utter and Gwendolyn Bridges Needham, *Pamela's Daughters* (New York: Macmillan, 1936; reprint ed., New York: Russell and Russell, 1972), p. 19.

5. John G. Cawelti, *Adventure, Mystery, and Romance: Formula Stories As Art and Popular Culture* (Chicago: University of Chicago Press, 1976), p. 41.

6. G. Richard Thompson, ed., *Romantic Gothic Tales, 1790-1840* (New York: Harper and Row, Perennial Library, 1979), p. 6.

7. Margot Northey, *The Haunted Wilderness: The Gothic and the Grotesque in Canadian Fiction* (Toronto: University of Toronto Press, 1976), pp. 13-14.

8. William Charvat, *Literary Publishing in America, 1790-1850* (Philadelphia: University of Pennsylvania Press, 1959), p. 23.

BIBLIOGRAPHY

Arvin, Newton. "Melville and the Gothic Novel." In *American Pantheon*. New York: Delacorte, 1966.

Bank, Stanley, ed. *American Romanticism: A Shape for Fiction.* New York: G. P. Putnam's Sons, 1969.

Baym, Nina. *Woman's Fiction: A Guide to Novels By and About Women in America, 1820-1870.* Ithaca, N.Y.: Cornell University Press, 1978.

Beer, Gillian. *The Romance.* London: Methuen, 1970.

Bell, Michael Davitt. *Hawthorne and the Historical Romance of New England.* Princeton, N.J.: Princeton University Press, 1971.

————. "History and Romance Convention in Catharine Sedgwick's *Hope Leslie.*" *American Quarterly* 22 (Summer 1970): 213-21.

Benson, Mary Sumner. *Women in Eighteenth-Century America.* New York: Columbia University Press, 1935. Reprint. New York: AMS Press, 1976.

Bettelheim, Bruno. *The Uses of Enchantment: The Meaning and Importance of Fairy Tales.* New York: Alfred A. Knopf, 1976.

Birkhead, Edith. "Sentiment and Sensibility in the Eighteenth-Century Novel." In *Essays and Studies by Members of the English Association,* collected by Oliver Elton, 11: 92-116. Oxford: The Clarendon Press, 1925.

————. *The Tale of Terror.* New York: Dutton, 1921. Reprint. New York: Russell and Russell, 1963.

Blakey, Dorothy. *The Minerva Press, 1790-1820.* London: Oxford University Press, 1939.

Bode, Carl. *The Anatomy of American Popular Culture, 1840-1861.* Berkeley: University of California Press, 1959.

Bogard, Robert. "Amelia Barr, Augusta Evans Wilson, and the Sentimental Novel." *Marab* 2 (Winter 1965-66): 13-25.

Brown, Herbert Ross. *The Sentimental Novel in America, 1789-1860.* Durham, N.C.: Duke University Press, 1940. Reprint. New York: Octagon Books, 1975.

Cantor, Norman, and Michael Wertham, eds. *History of Popular Culture.* 2 vols. New York: Macmillan, 1968.

Carrier, Esther J. *Fiction in Public Libraries, 1876-1900.* New York: Scarecrow Press, 1965.

Cawelti, John G. *Adventure, Mystery, and Romance: Formula Stories As Art and Popular Culture.* Chicago: University of Chicago Press, 1976.

Cecil, Mirabel. *Heroines in Love, 1750-1974.* London: Michael Joseph, 1974.

Charvat, William. *Literary Publishing in America, 1790-1850.* Philadelphia: University of Pennsylvania Press, 1959.

Chase, Richard. *The American Novel and Its Tradition.* Garden City, N.Y.: Doubleday, Anchor, 1957.

Clark, Kenneth. *The Gothic Revival: An Essay in the History of Taste.* New York: Holt, Rinehart, Winston, 1928. Reprint. New York: Humanities Press, 1970.

Coad, Oral Sumner. "The Gothic Element in American Literature Before 1835." *Journal of English and Germanic Philology* 24 (January 1925): 72-93.

Conrad, Susan P. *Perish the Thought: Intellectual Women in Romantic America, 1830-1860.* New York: Oxford University Press, 1976.

Cornillon, Susan Koppelman, ed. *Images of Women in Fiction: Feminist Perspectives.* Bowling Green, Ohio: Bowling Green State University Press, 1972.

Cott, Nancy F. *The Bonds of Womanhood: "Woman's Sphere" in New England, 1780-1835.* New Haven, Conn.: Yale University Press, 1977.

Cowie, Alexander. *The Rise of the American Novel.* 1948. Reprint. New York: American Book Co., 1951.

_____. "The Vogue of the Domestic Novel." *South Atlantic Quarterly* 41 (October 1942): 416-25.

Daiches, David. "The Novel As a Reflection of Middle-Class Attitudes." In *History of Popular Culture,* edited by Norman Cantor and Michael Wertham, vol. 1. New York: Macmillan, 1968. Excerpt from *A Critical History of English Literature.* 2 volumes. New York: Ronald Press, 1960.

Davidoff, Leonore. *The Best Circles: Society, Etiquette, and the Season.* London: Croom Helm, 1973.

Deegan, Dorothy Yost. *The Stereotype of the Single Woman in American Novels: A Social Study with Implications for the Education of Women.* New York: King's Crown Press, 1951. Reprint. New York: Octagon Books, 1969.

Douglas, Ann. *The Feminization of American Culture.* New York: Alfred A. Knopf, 1978.

_____. "Soft-Porn Culture." *New Republic* 183 (30 August 1980): 25- 29.

Ellmann, Mary. *Thinking About Women.* New York: Harcourt, Brace, Jovanovich, 1968.

Exman, Eugene. *The Brothers Harper.* New York: Harper and Row, 1965.

Fetterley, Judith. *The Resisting Reader: A Feminist Approach to American Fiction.* Bloomington, Ind.: Indiana University Press, 1978.

Fiedler, Leslie A. *Love and Death in the American Novel.* New York: Criterion, 1960. Reprint. New York: Dell, 1966.

Frederick, John T. "Hawthorne's 'Scribbling Women.' " *New England Quarterly* 48 (June 1975): 231-40.

Garrison, Dee. "Immoral Fiction in the Late Victorian Library." *American Quarterly* 28 (Spring 1976): 71-89.

Gilbert, Sandra M., and Susan Gubar. *The Madwoman in the Attic: The Woman Writer and the Nineteenth-Century Literary Imagination.* New Haven, Conn.: Yale University Press, 1979.

Haining, Peter, comp. *Gothic Tales of Terror.* 2 vols. Baltimore: Penguin Books, 1972.

Hardwick, Elizabeth. *Seduction and Betrayal: Women and Literature.* New York: Random House, 1974.

Hart, James D. *The Popular Book: A History of America's Literary Taste.* New York: Oxford University Press, 1950. Reprint. Westport, Conn.: Greenwood Press, 1976.

Hartman, Mary, and Lois W. Banner, eds. *Clio's Consciousness Raised.* New York: Harper and Row, 1974. Reprint. New York: Octagon Books, 1976.

Hoekstra, Ellen. "The Pedestal Myth Reinforced: Women's Magazine Fiction, 1900-1920." In *New Dimensions in Popular Culture,* edited by Russel B. Nye, pp. 43-58. Bowling Green, Ohio: Bowling Green State University Popular Press, 1972.

Hofstadter, Beatrice. "Popular Culture and the Romantic Heroine." *American Scholar* 30 (Winter 1960-61): 96-116.

Holman, C. Hugh. "Cheap Books and the Public Interest: Paperbound Book Publishing in Two Centuries." In *Frontiers of American Culture,* edited by Ray B. Browne et al., pp. 25-40. Lafayette, Ind.: Purdue University Press, 1968.

Hume, Robert D. "Gothic Versus Romantic: A Revaluation of the Gothic Novel." *PMLA* 84 (March 1969): 282-90.

_____. Introduction to *Longsword, Earl of Salisbury,* by Thomas Leland. New York: Arno Press, 1974.

_____, and Robert L. Platzner. "Gothic v. Romantic: A Rejoinder." *PMLA* 86 (March 1971): 266-74.

Kelley, Mary. "The Sentimentalists: Promise and Betrayal in the Home." *Signs* 4 (Spring 1979): 434-46.

Kiely, Robert. *The Romantic Novel in England.* Cambridge, Mass.: Harvard University Press, 1972.

Koch, Donald A. Introduction to *Tempest and Sunshine,* by Mary Jane Holmes, and *The Lamplighter,* by Maria Susanna Cummins. New York: Odyssey Press, 1968.

Lehman-Haupt, H., L. C. Wroth, and Rollo Silver. *The Book in America.* New York: R. R. Bowker, 1952.

Lieberman, Marcia R. " 'Some Day My Prince Will Come': Female Acculturation Through the Fairy Tale." *College English* 34 (1972): 383-95.

Long, O. W. "Werther in America." In *Studies in Honor of John Albrecht Walz.* Lancaster, Pa.: Lancaster Press, 1941. Reprint. Freeport, N.Y.: Books for Libraries Press, 1968.

Loshe, Lily D. *The Early American Novel, 1789-1830.* New York: Columbia University Press, 1907. Reprint. New York: Frederick Ungar, 1966.

Lundblad, Jane. *Nathaniel Hawthorne and the Tradition of the Gothic Romance.* Cambridge, Mass.: Harvard University Press, 1946. Reprint. New York: Haskell House, 1964.

McCarthy, Mary. "Can There Be a Gothic Literature?" Johan Huizinga Lecture. Amsterdam: Uitgeverij De Harmonie, 1973.

McGrath, Kathleen Conway. "Popular Literature as Social Reinforcement: The Case of *Charlotte Temple.*" In *Images of Women in Fiction: Feminist Perspectives,* edited by Susan Koppelman Cornillon. Bowling Green, Ohio: Bowling Green State University Press, 1972.

Madison, Charles A. *Book Publishing in America.* New York: McGraw-Hill, 1966.

Malin, Irving. *New American Gothic.* Carbondale, Ill.: Southern Illinois University Press, 1962.

Manley, Seon, and Gogo Lewis. *Ladies of the Gothic: Tales of Romance and Terror Told by the Gentle Sex.* New York: Lothrop, Lee, & Shephard, 1975.

_____. *Mistresses of Mystery: Two Centuries of Suspense Stories by the Gentle Sex.* New York: Lothrop, Lee, & Shepard, 1973.

Mayo, Robert D. Introduction to *Grasville Abbey,* by George Moore. New York: Arno Press, 1974.

Medlicott, Alexander, Jr. "The Legend of Lucy Brewer: An Early American Novel." *New England Quarterly* 39 (December 1966): 461-73.

Middendorp, Gerarda Maria Kooiman-von. *The Hero in the Feminine Novel.* Middelburg, Netherlands: Firma G. W. Den Boer, 1931. Reprint. New York: Haskell House, 1966.

Miller, William. *The Book Industry.* New York: Columbia University Press, 1949.

Mise, Raymond Winfield. "The Gothic Heroine and the Nature of the Gothic Novel." Ph.D. dissertation, University of Washington, 1970.

Mitchell, Sally. "The Forgotten Women of the Period: Penny Weekly Family Magazines of the 1840s and 1850s." In *A Widening Sphere,* edited by Martha Vicinus. Bloomington, Ind.: Indiana University Press, 1977.

_____. "Sentiment and Suffering: Women's Recreational Reading in the 1860s." *Victorian Studies* 21 (Autumn 1977): 29-45.

Miyoshi, Masao. *The Divided Self: A Perspective on the Literature of the Victorians.* New York: New York University Press, 1969.

Moebius, Hans. *The Gothic Romance.* Leipzig: Buchdruckerie, Grimme, and Treomel, 1902.

Moers, Ellen. *Literary Women.* Garden City, N.Y.: Doubleday, 1976.

Mott, Frank Luther. *Golden Multitudes.* New York: Macmillan, 1947.

Mussell, Kay J. "Beautiful and Damned: The Sexual Woman in Modern Gothic Fiction." *Journal of Popular Culture* 9 (Summer 1975): 84-89.

_____. "The World of Modern Gothic Fiction: American Women and Their Social Myths." Ph.D. dissertation, University of Iowa, 1973.

Nelson, Lowry, Jr. "Night Thoughts on the Gothic Novel." *Yale Review* 52 (December 1962): 236-57.

Noel, Mary. *Villains Galore: The Heyday of the Popular Story Weekly.* New York: Macmillan, 1954.

Northey, Margot. *The Haunted Wilderness: The Gothic and the Grotesque in Canadian Fiction.* Toronto: University of Toronto Press, 1976.

Nye, Russel B. *The Unembarrassed Muse.* New York: Dial, 1970.

_____, ed. *New Dimensions in Popular Culture.* Bowling Green, Ohio: Bowling Green State University Popular Press, 1972.

Orians, G. H. "Censure of Fiction in American Magazines and Romances, 1789-1810." *PMLA* 52 (March 1937): 195-214.

Papashvily, Helen W. *All the Happy Endings.* New York: Harper, 1956. Reprint. Port Washington, N.Y.: Kennikat Press, 1972.

Parker, Gail Thain, ed. *The Oven Birds: American Women on Womanhood, 1820-1920.* Garden City, N.Y.: Doubleday, 1972.

Pattee, Fred L. *The Feminine Fifties.* New York: Appleton-Century, 1940.

Peterson, Clell T. "Spotting the Gothic Novel." *Graduate Student of English* 1 (1957): 14-15.

Peterson, M. Jeanne. "The Victorian Governess: Status Incongruence in Family and Society." In *Suffer and Be Still,* edited by Martha Vicinus. Bloomington, Ind.: Indiana University Press, 1972.

Petter, Henri. *The Early American Novel.* Columbus, Ohio: Ohio State University Press, 1971.

Phillips, George L. "The Gothic Element in the American Novel Before

1830." *West Virginia University Bulletin: Philological Studies* 3 (September 1939): 37-45.

Quinn, Arthur Hobson. *American Fiction: An Historical and Critical Survey.* 1936. Reprint. New York: Appleton-Century-Crofts, 1964.

Railo, Eino. *The Haunted Castle.* London: Routledge, 1927. Reprint. New York: Gordon Press, 1974.

Ranieri, Marietta R. "The Self Behind the Self: The Americanization of the Gothic." Ph.D. dissertation, Pennsylvania State University, 1973.

Redden, Sister Mary Mauritia. *The Gothic Fiction in the American Magazines, 1765-1800.* Washington, D.C.: Catholic University Press, 1939.

Reynolds, Quentin. *The Fiction Factory.* New York: Random House, 1955.

Riley, Glenda Gates. "The Subtle Subversion: Changes in the Traditional Images of the American Woman." *The Historian* 32 (February 1970): 210-27.

Robinson, Lillian S. "On Reading Trash." In *Sex, Class, and Culture,* pp. 200-222. Bloomington, Ind.: Indiana University Press, 1978.

Russ, Joanna. "What Can a Heroine Do? or, Why Women Can't Write." In *Images of Women in Fiction: Feminist Perspectives,* edited by Susan Koppelman Cornillon. Bowling Green, Ohio: Bowling Green State University Press, 1972.

Ryan, Mary. "American Society and the Cult of Domesticity." Ph.D. dissertation, University of California at Santa Barbara, 1971.

Sadleir, Michael. " 'All Horrid?': Jane Austen and the Gothic Romance." In *Things Past,* pp. 167-200. London: Constable, 1944.

Satterthwaite, Joseph. "The Tremulous Formula: Form and Technique in *Godey's* Fiction." *American Quarterly* 8 (Summer 1956): 99-113.

Shove, Raymond H. *Cheap Book Production in the United States, 1870-1891.* Urbana, Ill.: University of Illinois Press, 1937.

Showalter, Elaine. *The Female Tradition in the English Novel: From Charlotte Brontë to Doris Lessing.* Princeton, N.J.: Princeton University Press, 1976.

Sklar, Kathryn Kish. *Catharine Beecher: A Study in American Domesticity.* New Haven, Conn.: Yale University Press, 1973.

Smith, H. "Feminism and the Household Novel." *Saturday Review* 40 (30 March 1957): 22.

Smith, Henry Nash. *Democracy and the Novel.* New York: Oxford University Press, 1978.

_____. "The Scribbling Women and the Cosmic Success Story." *Critical Inquiry* 1 (September 1974): 47-70.

_____. *Virgin Land: The American West in Symbol and Myth.* Cambridge, Mass.: Harvard University Press, 1950.

Smith, Leslie. "Through Rose-Colored Glasses: Some American Victorian Sentimental Novels." In *New Dimensions in Popular Culture,* edited by Russel B. Nye, pp. 90-106. Bowling Green, Ohio: Bowling Green State University Popular Press, 1972.

Smith-Rosenberg, Carroll. "The Female World of Love and Ritual: Relations Between Women in Nineteenth-Century America." *Signs* 1 (1975): 1-30.

Spacks, Patricia Meyer. "Ev'ry Woman Is at Heart a Rake." *Eighteenth-Century Studies* 8 (Fall 1974): 27-46.

————. *The Female Imagination.* New York: Alfred A. Knopf, 1975.

Spector, Robert Donald, ed. *Seven Masterpieces of Gothic Horror.* New York: Bantam, 1963.

Stearns, Bertha-Monica. "Before Godey's." *American Literature* 2 (November 1930): 248-55.

————. "Early New England Magazines for Ladies." *New England Quarterly* 2 (July 1929): 420-57.

Summers, Montague. *The Gothic Quest.* London: Fortune, 1938. Reprint. New York: Russell and Russell, 1964.

Tebbel, John Williams. *A History of Book Publishing in the United States.* 3 vols. New York: R. R. Bowker, 1972.

Thompson, G. Richard. "Introduction: Gothic Fiction in the Romantic Age: Context and Mode." In *Romantic Gothic Tales, 1790-1840,* pp. 1-54. New York: Harper and Row, Perennial Library, 1979.

Thompson, Gary R., ed. *The Gothic Imagination: Essays in Dark Romanticism.* Pullman, Wash.: Washington State University Press, 1974.

Thomson, Patricia R. *The Victorian Heroine, A Changing Ideal.* London: Oxford University Press, 1956.

Tompkins, J. M. S. *The Popular Novel in England, 1770-1800.* 1932. Reprint. London: Methuen, 1969.

Utter, Robert Palfrey, and Gwendolyn Bridges Needham. *Pamela's Daughters.* New York: Macmillan, 1936. Reprint. New York: Russell and Russell, 1972.

Varma, Devendra P. *The Gothic Flame.* 1957. Reprint. New York: Russell and Russell, 1966.

————, ed. *Gothic Novels.* 40 vols. New York: New York Times/Arno, 1971-.

Vicinus, Martha, ed. *Suffer and Be Still: Women in the Victorian Age.* Bloomington, Ind.: Indiana University Press, 1972.

————. *A Widening Sphere: Changing Roles of Victorian Women.* Bloomington, Ind.: Indiana University Press, 1977.

Wagenknecht, Edward. *Cavalcade of the American Novel.* New York: Holt, Rinehart and Winston, 1952.

Ward, Robert J. "Europe in American Historical Romances, 1890-1910." *Midcontinent American Studies Journal* 8 (Spring 1967): 90-97.

Wassertrom, William. *Heiress of All the Ages: Sex and Sentiment in the Genteel Tradition.* Minneapolis: University of Minnesota Press, 1959.

Watt, William W. *Shilling Shockers of the Gothic School: A Study of Chapbook Gothic Romances.* Cambridge, Mass.: Harvard University Press, 1932. Reprint. New York: Russell and Russell, 1967.

Weibel, Kathryn. *Mirror, Mirror: Images of Women Reflected in Popular Culture.* Garden City, N.Y.: Doubleday, Anchor, 1977.

Weiss, Harry B. *A Book About Chapbooks: The People's Literature of Bygone Times.* Ann Arbor, Mich.: Edwards Brothers, 1942. Reprint. Hatboro, Pa.: Folklore Associates, 1969.

Welter, Barbara. "The Cult of True Womanhood." *American Quarterly* 18 (Summer 1966): 151-74.

_____. *Dimity Convictions: The American Woman in the Nineteenth Century.* Athens, Ohio: Ohio University Press, 1976.

Wood, Ann D. "Mrs. Sigourney and the Sensibility of Inner Space." *New England Quarterly* 45 (June 1972): 163-81.

_____. "The 'Scribbling Women' and Fanny Fern: Why Women Wrote." *American Quarterly* 23 (Spring 1971): 3-24.

Yankelovich, Skelly, and White, Inc. *Consumer Research Study on Reading and Book Purchasing.* The Book Industry Study Group, Inc., October, 1978.

PERIODICALS

Publishers Weekly. New York: R. R. Bowker, 1872-.

CHAPTER 5

Sociological and Psychological Approaches to Gothic and Romantic Fiction: Studies of Reading and Audience

Gothic and romantic fiction, along with other formulas of popular entertainment, have been largely neglected by scholars, at least partly because of the difficulty of the analytical problems in working with such material. It is possible, of course, to find fine narrowly conceived disciplinary studies on such writers and works, but the task of synthesis has not been adequately articulated or carried out. As indicated previously, literary scholars have looked down upon popular gothic and romantic fiction on aesthetic grounds, historians use the material for illustration, and sociologists often use content analysis in evaluating it. None of these approaches, taken singly, takes into account the necessity of recognizing the essentially internal, private experience between a reader and a work that is the core of the meaning of such fiction in the lives of readers and in the cultural experience shared over two centuries by some American women. Some authors, to be sure, have attempted such syntheses and some have made contributions to our understanding of the fiction and of American women. But it seems unlikely that any study can go very far toward interpretation of the significance of this fictional pattern without two necessary preconditions: (1) an acknowledgment that the real meaning of such fiction is in its pervasive but relatively private appeal to women readers over time, and (2) some attempt to come to terms with sociological and psychological studies of women in America as well as with the small amount of research data that exists on the subject of the process of reading.

Literary studies of such writers as E. D. E. N. Southworth are unlikely to reveal any inherent aesthetic qualities in her works. She is, in our modern terms, such a laughable writer that an attempt to evaluate her in accepted critical fashion is fruitless, boring, and predictable. On the other hand, a strictly historical approach to her work might reveal interesting biographical data and background, but relatively little about her appeal to her readers. Attempts to blend historical and literary scholarship would probably result in antiquarianism. In fact, except for a very few authors of gothic and romantic fiction, it is probably less than useful to approach these authors individually. As Nina Baym recognizes, it is the type of fiction, the fact that a number of women writers and women readers converged on the same fictional pattern over a long period of time, that is significant.

On the other hand, sociological and psychological approaches lack the advantages of literary and historical insight. The sociologist or psychologist studies the people (or person), and readers in the past are, of course, unavailable, as are writers. If social scientists look at the works of fiction themselves, they tend to avoid evaluation of aesthetic or historical issues and, although they may be able to set forth interesting hypotheses, they often ignore the important issue of not just whether, what, and how often someone reads, but *how a reader reads.*

Another limited theoretical approach is that of library scientists, who are interested in the delivery and use of books. Certainly, library science studies provide excellent data on reader preferences over time, but since they focus upon public policy implications for library acquisitions and circulation, these studies do not attempt to approach the issue of reader preference on deeper sociopsychological and aesthetic levels.

When genuine theoretical scholarship on women's gothic and romantic fiction comes of age, it will be through a synthesis of these approaches: using the data compiled by librarians and booksellers and pollsters, in historical context, framed by the insights of psychologists concerned with male/female differences in development and role formation, placed in the context of socialization, but with a recognition of that essentially aesthetic experience, however repetitive, that occurs between reader and book and between readers and books over time. It is not an easy task, but this chapter suggests an approach to the fiction by turning the question around: instead of looking at authors and books, we need to also look at readers, their roles, and their motivations. It is in this that the research and insights of social scientists are crucial to our understanding of women's popular fiction.

Hypotheses about the interaction between reader and book must be complex. It is not enough to assume that a reader identifies in a straightforward way with the world of the fiction and the woman protagonist in any individual book, although that may be the case in some instances. But an attempt to draw a one-to-one comparison between world of reader and world of fiction fails from the outset. The lives of women in these novels, unlike the lives of readers, are not mundane, everyday affairs. Those lives are finite: the fiction gives them a beginning and an ending, a package into which all events and emotions can be wrapped. That package can be evaluated according to a conventional scheme. It is not simply that events in women's fiction are more exciting than those of everyday life, although that is surely true. The issue is that the world of fiction gives those exciting events a significance that is immediate and certain, a judgment of their quality and power that is much more secure than it could ever be in human life. In a gothic novel, the combination of mystery and romance has a specific and integrated significance within the fiction and, presumably, in the reader's mind as well. When the heroine escapes from or triumphs over the danger and wins the unequivocal love of the hero, a predictable and inevitable value configuration has been reaffirmed for the reader: virtue and courage within this fictional situation lead to the ultimate reward. In everyday life, of course, such events, when they occur, are much less amenable to ascription of value. Dangerous experiences remain dangerous in memory, without the distancing quality that fiction provides. Love relationships are problematic and day-to-day in real life, never wrapped up into a package labeled "happily ever after," as they are in women's fiction.

On the other hand, an interpretation that too intensely emphasizes the escape qualities of the fiction is also unsatisfactory. It is probably true that readers read these books partly because the events they describe are out of the ordinary and the value system is predictable and certain. But to say that is to beg the question of the kind of adventure and the kind of value system that is so appealing to so many women. There must be a more complex and revealing way of looking at the fiction that will take into account the discrepancies between the reader's way of life and that of the book, the particular values that are reaffirmed, the reader's own sense of reality inside and outside the fiction, and the conditions of society that produce a readership for this fiction. Certainly, readers do not read gothic and romantic novels because they believe such events actually happen in real life to ordinary people; they must be aware of the distinction between fantasy and reality. Nor should we assume that readers read these books because they want to be, or be like, the characters. The insights of researchers into reading psychology and identification can aid us in understanding the process between reader and book. In a similar fashion, the work of sociologists and psychologists can tell us something about the way these readers live, the social forces that shape their lives, and the roles and motivations that inform their actions. In the case of gothic and romantic fiction, the audience is primarily female, primarily middle-class, and relatively literate and informed. Readership surveys reveal that these readers are "typical" women and the high sales figures imply that such books meet a real need among this group. While researchers may be contemptuous of the contents of this fiction in terms of their own reading and intellectual preferences, one cannot dismiss the fiction as the pacifier of hordes of ill-adjusted, overly romantic women without distorting the reality of this phenomenon in American life. There is no single study that reconciles all of these disparate and competing issues into a coherent theory about the fiction and its readers, but there are innumerable pieces of evidence from a variety of fields that reinforce these impressions.

In the last decade, popular culture studies have been increasingly available within academia, and researchers in the field have come from a variety of disciplines. One of the issues that continually dominates the discussion, or should—the discussion suffers when the issue is ignored—is how the critic is able to make assumptions about the effect of popular forms of entertainment on the audience without direct knowledge of the audience itself. The question is a fair one, but most of the solutions offered are not comprehensive. The problem is even more acute in the evaluation of audiences for fiction, since reading is a private activity and data is hard to collect. Since it is impossible to construct a cognitive map of the audience by reading the fiction alone, one cannot make ungrounded assumptions about who that audience is. Since surveys of readers (and even in-depth interviews) have not to date either asked the right questions or been able to do so, approaching the phenomenon from the point of view of the readers has been unsatisfying.

Reading is essentially a private activity and the experience of reading an absorbing book does not lend itself readily to articulate explanation. Readers know, without being able to describe, the intense involvement that comes with submersion in good fiction—just as viewers of films or listeners to music know the emotional satisfactions that can come from shutting out the everyday world and temporarily relinquishing oneself to an aesthetic experience. But researchers quickly learn that direct questioning of subjects about their aesthetic escape experiences reveals little or nothing about why they find it so compelling. The experience is ineffable, taking one out of oneself, but interruptible in that it does not destroy the subject's ability to function in the world when the reading experience is halted or terminated. Approaches through the fiction or through the readers also fail at another point, in that each of them tends to assume that the audience is monolithic, that a theory can apply to a *group* of readers without taking into account the individuality and separateness of readers and, indeed, the solitary nature of reading as an activity.

One study that recognizes the implications of this problem is John G. Cawelti's *Adventure, Mystery, and Romance,* a book that assumes a close and sophisticated reading of types of literary texts may provide insight into the relationship between reader and book. Cawelti, more than other theorists of popular fiction, takes the literary/aesthetic approach as far as it will go by his careful recognition that the focus of discussion must be on the aesthetic experience of reading fiction and by his realization that formulas that are especially popular with a wide audience over time are appealing to readers not because readers are all alike but because those particular formulas maximize the possible range of responses from individual readers through their relative complexity. Cawelti is also careful in his work to limit the areas of human life into which he fits his hypotheses. He does not ask of popular fiction that it provide insight into humankind; he suggests merely that a close consideration of the fiction in its social context tells us something about the parts of human experience that relate to escape and entertainment and the needs that all human beings have for such experiences, whether they choose to satisfy their needs through fiction or through some other form of activity. Cawelti uses the insights of psychologists judiciously and carefully throughout the book. Cawelti has given us the best analysis of popular narratives and the most tools for further study currently available.

From the opposite point of view, that of the social scientist, the best work on women's romances has been done by a British sociologist, Peter H. Mann, who has a long-standing interest in women's fiction that has produced a number of books and articles on readers. Mann's tools are the survey and statistics, and his studies carefully limit the applicability of the conclusions to particular issues. He does not attempt analysis of the literary or aesthetic qualities of the works; instead, he asks certain demographic questions of the readers and he intersperses the data with direct quotations from his respondents. What he provides is a partial portrait of the readers of romantic novels (in Britain) in their day-to-day lives, leaving evaluation of the reading and why they read to other researchers.

For the analysis of popular women's fiction, both Cawelti's work and Mann's work are essential sources, coming from opposite points on the spectrum, because their research is meticulous and of high quality, never claiming for itself more than it can do within the constraints of method. Taken together, they provide rich material for the approaches of other researchers. But between these two approaches, there is a more problematic but essential issue that has not to date been fully explored. Beginning with Cawelti's insistence that popular texts, in formulas, must be approached on their own terms and continuing with Mann's profile of women who read romances, the essential question may be asked: what is it in this type of fiction and about these particular readers that provides the bond between them? What needs and motivations are being satisfied? What causes the convergence of so many women around the world on a particular fictional world that can be chosen, absorbed, laid aside, and repeated through individual preferences and time schedules as a common, though solitary, experience?

If humanistic and social science approaches are both valuable and limited, a careful evaluation of the work that has been done in each to date might reveal the areas of need for investigation. There are several related assumptions that provide a basis for discussion:

1. Literary approaches say little about readers.
2. Readership surveys say little about the fiction.
3. Reader research, in all fields, is relatively undeveloped.
4. Readership surveys have not to date asked the questions that can bridge the gap, although the demographic data they provide is essential in understanding who the audience is.
5. Interviews alone cannot reveal the connection because the audience, like all audiences, is inarticulate.

An essay by Heinz Steinberg, "Books and Readers as a Subject of Research in Europe and America," provides a good point of departure. Steinberg critiques the current methods for research and their limitations by distinguishing between the salient approaches in America and Europe.

In the United States research into reading is generally carried out by librarians and sociologists as an advisory service to libraries. . . . Frequently it is directed almost exclusively to the practical needs of libraries, and the world of books outside tends to be overlooked. Research in Europe, mainly sponsored by booksellers and publishers, is empirical in nature and so, often commercially oriented and consequently biased in its findings.[1]

A publication for the British Library Board in 1977 provides support for Steinberg's contention. *The Reading Habits of Adults: A Selected*

Annotated Bibliography by Margaret Mann is an essential survey of sources on reading research since 1930. The study shows in list after list the strong bias of such work toward library and commercial studies. There are very few humanistic studies of reading, and very few of the annotations indicate that the study attempts to draw qualitative conclusions about adult reading habits.

For an example of good humanistic writing on reading in America, Roger H. Smith's *The American Reading Public* should be examined. The book is a collection of essays that originally appeared in *Daedalus* as a symposium, and it contains a fine survey of highbrow writing on the subject of American readers and their tastes. It has nothing of relevance to women's fiction, however.

Librarians have a particular viewpoint on popular reading. They are rarely interested in why certain readers read what they do, although librarians occasionally write interesting essays on what is happening in their branches or how they wish to raise the taste of their patrons. Margaret A. Kateley's "They Also Read Who Roll in Dough" is a sprightly article on her upper-middle-class patrons in a suburban library. K. F. Kister's "Of 'Luvs' and 'Lights' " is a typically wrongheaded attack on English librarians for failing to improve their readers' choice of books. A British essay, M. Pehle's "Readers' Tastes as Seen by a Mobile Librarian," chattily discusses a librarian's expriences. More useful than any of these is the report of a survey in the *Library Journal* in 1965. "Book Committee Chairman Reports Survey on Housewives' Reading" indicates that heavy readers read much more light fiction, such as mysteries, than do light readers, and are less specific about titles when asked what they have read in a recent period. This brief report fits well with other, more extensive, analyses of readers and their reading habits. Impressionistic as well as survey evidence would lead one to believe that people who define themselves as *readers* tend to read voraciously, one book after another, usually choosing predictable types of fiction, and that when they indicate their reading preferences they refer to types of books rather than to specific titles. It is probably true that these "heavy" readers make up the majority of the audience for women's romances as well as for other formulas of popular fiction. Evidence about the successful marketing techniques of series romances, such as Harlequin and its imitators, would also indicate that this observation is true.

Several years ago, the National Council of Teachers of English sponsored a report by Alan C. Purves and Richard Beach entitled *Literature and the Reader*. Although the book does not speak directly to the issue of women and reading, it does contain useful summaries of research.

John Cawelti called it "a handy survey and bibliography of psychological research on literary response, both Freudian and non-Freudian."[2] It is a good beginning source for psychological approaches.

A more sophisticated approach to reading taste is a suggestive article by Robert Oliphant entitled "Toward a Theory of Reading Sequence." Oliphant wants to increase reading in the United States because he assumes, along with so many other contemporary commentators, that reading is on the decline. This may not be true, as other researchers have shown, but the assumption informs most of the writing on this subject and must be dealt with. Oliphant notes in the essay that "we read what we read . . . because of what we are," and that "we read what we read because of what we have read."[3] Although both statements may seem simplistic, many writers on the subject of readers and reading do not take them for granted. Oliphant's contribution is the clear statement of that belief: reading is not manipulative, although the range of reading materials available may be dictated by commercial needs. People choose reading matter out of profound inner and individual motives based upon their own social and individual situations in life and their previous experience with other reading matter. If this were not true, we would not see the connection we do between demographic surveys and particular reading choices, nor would there be so many readers who choose books by author and type. Any librarian or bookseller will attest to the fact that certain types of readers choose certain types of books and that many requests for new reading material come in the form of requests for the latest book of a particular author or the latest example of a particular type of book.

Oliphant goes on to state something about the act of choosing a particular book, recognizing many of the issues that must be confronted in dealing with why women read gothic and romantic novels.

In clinical work, it has long been recognized that the act of reading plays a large part in developing a sense of identity. The act of reading, after all, is an act of choice: our man in the bookstore, as Walker Gibson has put it, is really deciding upon a choice of role, and his choice will undoubtedly shape the way he thinks about himself.[4]

Oliphant leaves to others the development of the implications of his assumptions, but he states them succinctly and well.

Robert Escarpit's *Sociology of Literature* addresses the issue of particular groups' reading tastes more directly, and he also has something to say about women's choice of romantic fiction over other types. Escarpit says that "the behavior of women readers seems more homogeneous than that of male readers."[5] Women readers, he reports, choose sentimental, historical, and detective novels frequently, and he suggests that this is true "on all levels of society."[6] He also believes that young women are more likely to read this kind of fiction than older ones since "the older a person becomes the more literary his reading—and this is true of both men and women."[7] Escarpit believes that young women choose this material more frequently because they are at an age "when *bovaryism* has a stronger hold" and that the relative homogeneity of their reading is related to the fact that "women's way of life is relatively uniform," thus assuming with Oliphant that reading choice is a product of individual and group experience and conditions.[8] "As to the particular kind of reading they choose," he goes on, "it goes back to the seventeenth and eighteenth centuries. Boredom, at a time when the social and political responsibilities of women were practically non-existent, was undoubtedly one of the sources of the romantic novel."[9]

A particularly relevant study for analysis of women's gothic and romantic fiction is Jan Hajda's "A Time for Reading." Hajda surveyed a number of women in Baltimore on the subject of their reading and their other leisure-time activities. The survey of 1722 readers was supported by the Enoch Pratt Free Library. The women were all married or widowed. Hajda discovered that if education was equal, there was no age differential in terms of reading habits. Older women read as much as younger women. Dividing his group into those who read and those who did not, he found that the readers had broad and frequent social contacts and that there was much discussion among friends of books and reading. Many of these readers frequently borrowed books and loaned their books to others. Interestingly, the women who were wives with children read more than those with no children. These women read, among other types of books, historical novels, love stories, suspense stories, and biographical novels; each of these types fits into the continuum of gothic and romantic women's fiction.

Hajda's study is especially valuable in its evidence that heavy readers of escape fiction for women are not abnormal. Beginning with a description of a movie stereotype of a woman with glasses, hair in a bun, reading and then magically transformed into a lovely object with no glasses, hair down, and in love—he could be describing Joan Fontaine in Hitchcock's *Suspicion*—Hajda says:

This movie stereotype exploits the common notion that book reading is a substitute for life and that people who read a lot tend to be withdrawn and lonely. But the truth is almost precisely the opposite. Quite different impressions of book readers emerged from a survey we conducted recently. . . . The study showed that social integration—having many active personal relationships with people outside one's immediate family—actually encourages and sustains regular reading. Isolation, in contrast, may led to a total abandonment of books.[10]

Hajda goes on to say that "more or less avid book reading, as described here, seems to be riding a paradox. The desire to read is associated both with gregariousness and with opportunity and desire for solitude. The act of book reading simultaneously requires a fair degree of social integration and of individual autonomy. Reading deepens contact with humanity, rather than drawing away from it."[11]

Hajda's work, limited though it is, is highly significant for analysis of women's popular fiction because he places readers of such work firmly within the range of normal, happy, reasonably well adjusted human beings, suggesting in fact that there is something revitalizing and healthy about avid reading. Unlike critics who assume that compulsive readers read because they lack so much in their lives and they use reading as a poor substitute for experience to fill the empty spaces, Hajda would lead us to believe that reading is an alternative form of experiencing life that promotes good social relationships and equilibrium no matter how formulaic the reading experience. Although he does not address the issue as such, he points the way toward psychological studies of the reading experience and allows us, as Cawelti would wish us to do, to take into account the aesthetic nature of the reading experience itself whether we approve of the contents of the book or not. Hajda allows us to get away from the pejorative assumptions of negative influence of particular types of books by suggesting that there is something in the reading experience itself that is important to examine. Only after examining that dynamic relationship can we begin to try to understand why particular types of readers choose particular types of books.

Further evidence for the utility of such an approach comes from a remarkably useful recent commercial study commissioned by the Book Industry Study Group. In October, 1978, the polling firm of Yankelovich, Skelly, and White interviewed 1450 people in America over the age of sixteen. Interviews were random but the surveyors closely approximated the demographic profile of the census in selecting subjects. Researchers will be mining this study for years, but the most significant findings for purposes of studying the audience for popular reading were those that contradicted assumptions and stereotypes that had been held by many scholars in the past. The Yankelovich group found that reading was not declining in America and that many more people than had previously been suppposed actually chose to read books and to read often. The survey reports that 94 percent of Americans read voluntarily but that only 25 percent are involved in book reading to a great extent. The data breaks down as follows.

—6 percent of the population do not read (nonreaders);
—39 percent of the population do not read books, but do read shorter items (nonbook readers);
—55 percent of the population read books;
—30 percent are "light" book readers, reading between one and nine books in the six months prior to the interview; and
—25 percent are moderate to heavy book readers, reading more than ten books in that same period.[12]

Yankelovich reports that there are no significant regional distinctions. Book readers often describe their reading as done for pleasure, defined as "a deep sense of reward and satisfaction."[13] Those who read books find that they can fit books into very heavy schedules and that they make distinctions between kinds of reading, calling fiction their reading for pleasure and nonfiction their reading for knowledge. Nonbook readers, on the other hand, profess to not have time for reading and they define themselves as readers for knowledge.[14] There are strong indications that "the heaviest book readers are more likely than others to have read books in *nearly all* fiction categories."[15] Although many researchers have assumed that reading is declining because of the availability of television, this survey says that television is not directly competitive with reading. Those who read books watch as much television as those who do not read books.[16]

Aggregating the data, the report shows that "consistently heavy readers are more likely (relative to those with other reading histories) to be [a] women, [b] housewives, [c] age 30-59 (and less likely to be under 30), [d] college graduates, [e] white, and [f] in the highest income brackets."[17] It is tempting to suggest that that is also a profile of women readers of gothic and romantic fiction, but such a conclusion would be unwarranted at this point. Yankelovich also points out that "women are predominantly *leisure* readers."[18] Echoing Hajda, whose work the survey cites, the researchers discovered that the stereotype of the bookworm is inaccurate in describing heavy book readers. "Book readers, particularly heavier volume ones, are *not* solitary people. They have the greatest involvement in other leisure time activities—'the doers are the doers.' "[19] And like Hajda, the survey discovered that women with small children in the household are more likely rather than less likely to be heavy readers, although among women without children those who work outside the home are more likely to read than those who do not.

Since this survey was done for the benefit of the book industry, there is much data about how people obtain books to read. Yankelovich points out that among readers there is what he calls a ''strong informal 'pass along' factor when it comes to books—with heavier readers helping to keep lighter readers in the market.''[20] He adds: ''The *word-of-mouth* factor in book selections cannot be underplayed. Book readers rely very heavily on *recommendations of friends* in selecting books.''[21] Only 16 percent of book readers belong to book clubs and, on the average, those who belong purchase about one book each month from the clubs.[22]

Identified as major categories of choice in fiction are action/adventure, historical novels, mystery and detective novels, short stories, modern dramatic novels, and romantic/gothic novels. Much of the data is based upon preferences for these kinds of books, so there is a wealth of information on women readers who choose gothic and romantic fiction. Twenty-seven percent of book readers express their interest in reading gothic and romantic novels. Of these, 44 percent had read more than twenty-five in the previous six months; 28 percent had read between ten and twenty-five; 24 percent, between four and nine; and 15 percent, between one and three.[23] In addition, among readers of gothic and romantic fiction, the average number read in six months is nine, a very high average for any type of book. Twelve percent of readers purchase gothic and romantic novels, and they averaged seventeen dollars in six months on such purchases, again a very high average for any kind of book.[24]

From another vantage point, Yankelovich points out that ''certain fiction categories . . . elicit readership of a relatively large *number* of books (on the average, among readers in the particular category). These include:

Juvenile/children's fiction
Romantic/Gothic novels
Mysteries/detective stories
Westerns.''[25]

Similarly, some fiction categories are particularly noteworthy for the number of copies actually purchased rather than borrowed by readers who prefer them. ''These include Gothic/romantic novels and juvenile/children's fiction. Per-person expenditures (among purchasers) for Gothic novels and juvenile fiction are also among the highest of all fiction categories."[26] Clearly, those women who do choose to read gothic and romantic fiction are devoted readers who take time and go to expense to satisfy their interest.

The Yankelovich survey, of course, covers much more than this, but as a source for hard data on readers of gothic and romantic fiction, it cannot be equalled. It supports certain hypotheses about the novels, rejects others that have been long accepted, and points the way toward numerous follow-up studies that could be done. In the fall of 1978, the Center for the Book at the Library of Congress sponsored a symposium based upon the findings of the Yankelovich, Skelly, and White survey. The proceedings of that symposium were edited by John Y. Cole and Carol S. Gold and published by the Library of Congress in a volume entitled *Reading in America, 1978*. In addition to an abbreviated summary of the survey's findings, the book contains opening statements by commentators (including Barbara Tuchman), a summary of previous research, a bibliography, and a summary of seminar participants' comments about the survey. In an appendix, the volume summarizes the results of a poll conducted by Gallup for the American Library Association. The study of libraries and reading covered such issues as use of libraries, increase of library services, a demography of library users, information on American reading preferences, and comments about the effects of television on reading. The brief summary of this poll supports the results of the Yankelovich survey. For information on gothic and romantic fiction, its most significant findings were that the public's favorite types of novels are "romantic novels, like *The Thorn Birds* by Colleen McCullough, and historical romances."[27] The survey also notes that bestsellers from the past are still popular, and it specifically mentions *Gone With the Wind* and *Rebecca*, romantic or gothic, as favorite reading. Researchers will find that the full report of the Yankelovich survey is essential, but the summary and comments of the Library of Congress symposium are also helpful.

If Hajda and Yankelovich serve to place reading of gothic and romantic fiction in some perspective, the work of Peter H. Mann in Great Britain sharpens the picture. Mann's interest in reading is in reading habits and in the demographic profiles of particular kinds of readers that support an understanding of those habits. He has worked, occasionally, in research commissioned by commercial publishers. The data must be used with caution since his research was conducted in Great Britain and not in America, but the clear congruence between his reader profiles for romantic fiction in Great Britain and the reader profiles in the Yankelovich survey in America suggests that his data may be applicable to America as well.

Some of Mann's work centers upon booksellers and the sociological aspects of book reading and are not directly relevant to the study of romantic fiction, but these studies are still important for setting his work on romantic fiction in context. *Books and Reading* by Mann and Jacqueline L. Burgoyne is a progress report on a survey of the sociological aspects of book reading in Britain. *Books: Buyers and Borrowers* studies book acquisition patterns. Chapter 5 is especially important since it discusses "Light Fiction and the Romantic Novel." Another study by Mann, *Bookselling: An Occupational Survey* is interesting but not relevant to romantic fiction.

Mann's major contribution, however, is in the reports of two mail surveys that he conducted for the British publishing firm of Mills and Boon. Mills and Boon is a phenomenon in British publishing. The firm specializes in the publication of light romances aimed at a female audience and distributed to readers directly as well as through bookstores and libraries. The most innovative marketing device of Mills and Boon in Great Britain and the Commonwealth nations has been its use of a mailing list to which the firm sends a regular catalog so that individual readers can order the books for themselves. The books are relatively inexpensive. Starting out as a series of "nurse" romances, Mills and Boon books evolved into straightforward and simple romantic novels with a clear and predictable formula of their own. They are simply love stories with perhaps a slight tinge of adventure or an exotic location. They are "clean" books, with all sexual reference banished or handled euphemistically. Over the past two decades, they have become phenomenally successful. If Mills and Boon had remained a British and Commonwealth firm, Mann's data might not seem so important for researchers on American women's reading habits. However, its Canadian affiliate, Harlequin Romances, has in the past several years made startling inroads on the fiction market in the United States. Harlequin's marketing techniques are as innovative as those of Mills and Boon.

Although Harlequin Romances are available in conventional book outlets, such as bookstores and grocery stores, their success in America seems to be more directly the result of their subscription series. Harlequin Romances are available by subscription to readers in America at a rate of $7.60 for eight books per month. With the books comes a magazine, *Harlequin*, containing routine women's magazine features, such as travel pieces and recipes, along with short stories and a complete additional novel. Expanding, Harlequin has added a series called Harlequin Presents, offering four novels per month for $5.00. A new Harlequin series is called Mystiques, and they are gothic novels. In addition, Harlequin offers books containing three back-issue novels by favorite Harlequin authors, Harlequin Historicals, and other repackagings of earlier books. This is, of course, a prolific output, but faithful readers are joining the series in large numbers. Sales figures for the past decade are remarkable: in 1972, Mills and Boon/Harlequin combined for sales of 27 million copies; in 1973, more than 30 million; in 1974, more than 40 million; and in 1978, 50 million. Even higher figures have been quoted in some trade sources. In the spring of 1979, Harlequin embarked on an aggressive advertising campaign, using television. Significantly, one of the first advertisements was shown during the television airing of *Gone With the Wind*. Until late 1979, Harlequin books were distributed in the United States by Simon and Schuster, but the arrangement was terminated when that firm established its own series of light romances, in the wake of similar American series by a variety of other publishers. All this indicates that the market for light romances is increasing in this country and that, once again, the British are leading the way in production of titles for the audience. Although early Harlequin Romances were reprints of British novels and had British or Commonwealth settings, recent Harlequins have been American or Canadian.

Mann's attitude toward women's romances is tolerant. He argues convincingly in *Books: Buyers and Borrowers* that such books fill a real need and should be taken seriously, and that the conventional condescending attitudes toward such leisure reading are inappropriate and based upon inaccurate conclusions about the readers. Much like Hajda, he discovered that the readers were a cross section of British women with significantly more education and better jobs and status than had been assumed. Mann surveyed readers in 1968 and 1973 by sending a coded questionnaire to the Mills and Boon mailing list, receiving more than twenty-seven hundred replies the first time and over two thousand the second. The response rate (almost 30 percent) was very high for a voluntary, mail-in survey, indicating a high level of reader interest, although Mann admitted that it was not a scientific survey. He assumed that the level of response was skewed toward the more highly educated reader. Results of both surveys were published by Mills and Boon. The first is *The Romantic Novel: A Survey of Reading Habits*; the second, *A New Survey: The Facts About Romantic Fiction*.

In both surveys, readers were overwhelmingly beyond the average age of first marriage and the majority were married already. In 1968, 59 percent were between the ages of twenty-five and fifty-four, tapering off sharply after forty-five—only 47 percent of British women in the 1966 census were in that age range.[28] In 1973, 64 percent of readers and 46 percent of British women were between twenty-five and fifty-four.[29] Mann comments in the first study, "It does seem reasonable to infer from this distribution that, rather than stopping reading on marriage as is expected of many book readers, the readers of Mills and Boon Romances actually increase in the years of marriage and raising of children."[30] The obvious question to ask is why women who are already married like to read romances about courtship and marriage. Mann suggests, "Being brought up in a society in which romantic love is stressed at an early age, they perhaps find that actuality is far from the rose-coloured dream they had expected and the Romance offers a vicarious form of experience."[31] This demographic data from Britain supports Yankelovich and Hajda at two major points: it shows a higher-than-expected age, occupation, and status combination for readers of light romances, and it suggests that readers of such fiction are not maladjusted bookworms substituting vicarious for real experience but fairly ordinary women who heighten their reality with vicarious experience.

The limitation of such demographic and reading studies, however, is apparent in the fact that their speculations about readers' motivations are tentative and not based upon theoretical principles. The bridge between humanistic and social science studies is not established without looking further into psychological approaches that help to explain concepts of identification, the role of fantasy in human life, and the crucial relationship between reader and book. Using psychological material is difficult because so little of it relates directly to the process of reading, but there are a few studies that are suggestive and should be consulted. For example, in a major study, *The Structure and Functions of Fantasy*, Eric Klinger provides much important information on daydreaming. Although daydreaming as a form of fantasy is not the same as reading fiction, which is an externally controlled form of fantasy, the age profile of daydreamers is significant when placed against the age profile of women readers described by Mann. Klinger asserts that active fantasy begins at the point in a person's life when active play ends, around the time of puberty; it peaks in late adolescence and early adulthood and then declines slowly. Such daydreams from prepubescence through early adulthood tend to be *prospective* and as they decline in adulthood, they become progressively less so. These fantasies anticipate the subject's future and as life choices narrow, so fantasy declines. Reading, on the other hand, increases, peaks, and declines slightly later in the life cycle. It is tempting to suggest that at the point where life options are being foreclosed through maturation and decision making, reading takes over by offering a substitute form of prospective fantasy that temporarily wipes out life choices already made and allows what Peter L. Berger and

Thomas Luckmann would call "world-openness" to obtain once more for the subject.

If the analogy between daydreams and the reading of fiction holds up, then further evaluation of the psychological data is appropriate. In a major study, *The Dynamics of Literary Response*, Norman N. Holland offers a sophisticated Freudian interpretation of the act of reading, relating it to a regression to infancy and dependency in which the reader is taken over by the fiction. He suggests that when people are involved in entertainment, they (1) "Cease to pay attention to what is outside the work of art," (2) "concentrate attention wholly on it," and (3) "begin to lose track of the boundaries between themselves and the work of art."[32] In other words, they immerse themselves in a different world through a process that, in terms of reading, we could call *identification*. Through shutting out the everyday, mundane world, readers identify with a dramatic, controlled, and heightened world of fantasy. They do not need to perform the mental tricks necessary for daydreams—for example, in order to experience romance anew, married women do not have to first imagine how they became single again—instead, they assume the fictional role of a protagonist with a different life history and with a different set of life options. Of course, this process is a finite one—it ends on the last page of the book—but through selection of formulaic literature, it is a repeatable experience. Harlequin Romances, to name just one of these formulaic series, maximize this process by offering so many books so easily. The Holland book contains much more information on literary response and is infinitely rewarding, although some readers may be wary because of his firm adherence to Freudian terminology and concepts. It is likely, in particular, that feminist researchers will be unreceptive to his approach, but they probably ignore it at their peril.

In fact, as several recent critics of Freud have noted, Freudian approaches to psychosexual development are badly understood, even among knowledgeable observers of culture. Christopher Lasch argues in *Haven in a Heartless World* that Freudian theory is not deterministic but descriptive of how femininity and masculinity develop in culture.[33] Juliet Mitchell, in *Psychoanalysis and Feminism*, reinforces the point. "Psychoanalysis does not describe what a woman is—far less what she should be; it can only try to comprehend how psychological femininity comes about."[34]

Since what seems to bother so many academic critics about women's romances is the passivity and vacuousness of the female protagonists of such books, their inability and lack of interest in assuming active roles in the world, and their willingness to subsume themselves in a man, waiting to be chosen and then drifting off into a "happily ever after" world, it may well be that psychoanalysis and other psychological approaches to women will bear discussion in connection with women's reading choices.

Among the materials that should be examined are recent psychological writings on women. Juliet Mitchell's *Psychoanalysis and Feminism* is a reinterpretation of Freud and others in terms of feminist scholarship. Several volumes on the psychology of women are recent enough to take into account feminist theory. Among these are Juanita H. Williams's *Psychology of Women: Behavior in a Biosocial Context*, Julia Sherman's *On the Psychology of Women: A Survey of Empirical Studies*, and Judith M. Bardwick's *Psychology of Women: A Study of Bio-Cultural Conflicts*. A book of collected essays, Bardwick's *Readings on the Psychology of Women*, is a fine source of recent short psychological studies. One should also look at the essays of Karen Horney, a disciple of Freud who broke with him partly over the issue of psychosexual development of the female. Phyllis Whitney has written that she uses Horney as a source for information on feminine psychology when she writes her gothic novels.[35] Horney's work is accessible in *Feminine Psychology*, edited by Harold Kelman.

Some of Freud's own writings are also important, especially in light of his revisions of his theories about women later in his life. The dates of specific essays are important, however, for he did not always hold the fairly repressive attitudes toward women of which he has been accused. Notably, his essay, "Family Romances of Neurotics," describes the fantasies of patients who wish they were members of more significant and powerful families and thus, in fantasy, substitute more romantic figures for their real fathers and mothers. Since this substitution is exactly what often occurs in women's romantic fiction— with the addition of more significant husbands and lovers through whom status can be ascribed—the concept is important.

Erik H. Erikson has also written extensively on psychosexual development of women, suggesting that the crucial point in a young girl's life is when she "relinquishes the care received from the parental family in order to commit herself to the love of a stranger and the care to be given to his or her offspring."[36] This crucial point for Erikson is the dramatic subject of almost all women's romantic fiction.

Another major psychological approach not limited to women but highly relevant is Bruno Bettelheim's *The Uses of Enchantment: The Meaning and Importance of Fairy Tales*. Many researchers have noted that the plot structure of women's romances is analogous to that of the major fairy tales, especially those compiled by the Brothers Grimm, on which many young women were raised. The Cinderella story, for example, is the basic structure of most romances, including the passive nature of the heroine, her selection by the prince because of her inherent virtues and beauty, its ending with marriage (the rest of her life is insignificant), and the rivalry with other women. Snow White, also, contains many of these elements as does the story of Sleeping Beauty. Bettelheim's analysis of these traditional tales increases our insight into the patterns of modern women's reading material and modern women's lives.

Although it would be impossible to survey recent psychological scholarship on women in a feminist context, one anthology of essays should be mentioned specifically. Rhoda Kesler Unger and Florence L. Denmark's *Woman: Dependent or Independent Variable?* contains a wide variety of essays on various aspects of the psychology of women. Most notable are a reprint of Viola Klein's 1950 essay, "The Stereotype of Femininity," in which she discusses some of the problems in stereotypical thinking especially in the sciences, and Helen K. Franzwa's "Female Roles in Women's Magazine Fiction, 1940-1970," a thematic content analysis in which her categories correspond to women's marital statuses. She asserts that the major themes in such fiction are that marriage is inevitable and women can learn how to keep a man.

Albert Ellis's essay, "Romantic Love," is an excellent description of the concept in psychosocial context. Drawing upon mass media stereotypes of romantic love, Ellis states: "Only in our own day, for the first time in history, has romantic love become ubiquitous. Whereas our forefathers expected only relatively few gentlemen and gentlewomen to love romantically, we expect every male and female to do so."[37] The mass media provide a prescription for proper romantic love, he says, that is very hard to find in real life. His lengthy description of that stereotype accords well with the value system of women's fiction.

Other important essays, variously useful, are mere samples of a vast field. Jean Lipman-Blumen's "How Ideology Shapes Women's Lives" reports the results of a survey of the "life plans of married women" and argues, as does Bardwick in her book-length *Readings on the Psychology of Women*, that women are encouraged to satisfy their achievement motivations vicariously through the men in their lives rather than through their own activities. This leads to the passivity evident in heroines of women's romances. J. Kagan's "The Concept of Identification," while not directly relevant to identification through fiction, stresses identification *behavior*, giving important background for an understanding of the psychological need to identify with others. An indication of how early our society begins to affect the psychological development of children can be found in J. Z. Rubin, F. J. Provenzano, and Z. Luria's "The Eye of the Beholder: Parent's Views on Sex of Newborns."

A number of sociologists have done studies of patterns in women's magazine fiction. The following list is not definitive, but suggests the range of studies. In 1938, Ruth Inglis's essay, "An Objective Approach to the Relationship Between Fiction and Sociology" used *Saturday Evening Post* stories to support a discussion of whether literature is a "reflection" of or an "influence" on society. Comparing heroines of love stories to the census data, Inglis concludes that the stories "reflect" society. This is a simplistic, although competent, study. In a much-reprinted classic study, Patricke Johns-Heine and Hans H. Gerth examined "Values in Mass Periodical Fiction, 1921-1940," a content analysis of stories from several popular magazines. Although it does not limit itself to women's stories, the study is a valuable one because it assumes that such stories provide models for readers and that those models are very limited ones. In a 1949 essay, Margaret Mead asked "Can Marriage Be For Life?" She argued that the American marriage pattern is one of the hardest to maintain, explaining why and how the myths about romantic marriage perpetrated by popular fiction can cause problems by encouraging people to feel disappointed in their own life situations. Margaret Bailey's survey, "The Women's Magazine Short-Story Heroine in 1957 and 1967," indicates that the magazines were even more conservative in the later year than in the earlier one on the subject of women's roles. There is little evidence of reaction to feminist thought, unless it is a simplistic response to Betty Friedan. "Working Women in Fact and Fiction" by Helen K. Franzwa is a simplistic survey of women's magazines showing that most women portrayed are housewives and saying that the magazines do not reflect social reality. A similar conclusion was reached by Marya G. Hatch and David L. Hatch in their 1958 essay, "Problems of Married and Working Women as Presented by Three Popular Working Women's Magazines." Surveying not the fiction but the advice articles aimed at working women in *Mademoiselle*, *Glamour*, and *Charm*, the Hatches conclude that the magazines try to help working women do everything well, and that they do not recognize either the conflicts between husbands' and wives' careers or the possible strains, physical and emotional, on women in such circumstances. A chapter in Betty Friedan's *The Feminine Mystique* argues that the images presented to women changed between the 1930s and 1950s, becoming more domestic and passive in the later period.

A recent collection of sociological essays edited by Gaye Tuchman, Arlene Kaplan Daniels, and James Benet is *Hearth and Home: Images of Women in the Mass Media*. Although there are no articles on women's romantic fiction, many of the essays in the book are relevant to it through their perceptive analysis of the roles of women in society. The book is written with a refreshing lack of jargon and contains a good selection of articles on women's roles as seen on television, in magazines, and in newspapers, along with an excellent bibliography of articles on women's images in television.

In the past decade, the women's studies movement in scholarship has brought a wide variety of studies of women in society. Often written from a feminist point of view, these studies have caused many changes in the ways scholars look at women and women's issues in America. A sample of some of those studies shows how ideas about American women are changing and suggests the context in which we might more fruitfully examine the implications of women's leisure reading. Of course, not all women referred to in these studies read romantic fiction; but all of the demographic data on readers shows that the audience for the fiction is virtually exclusively female. One cannot draw absolute conclusions based on social science studies of women relative to women's reading; on the other hand, such studies must not be ignored if one wishes to understand the social context of the reading and its background.

The book that is usually credited with beginning the contemporary feminist movement is Betty Friedan's *The Feminine Mystique*. Based on interviews with a number of well-educated housewives, the book describes these women's dissatisfactions with their life patterns. Friedan's book was meant for a popular audience, although it has been very influential on academic researchers as well. Another useful popular book is Caroline Bird's *Born Female: The High Cost of Keeping Women Down*, centering on the encouragement given by social institutions to women to keep them out of the work force, focussed on family and home, and out of instrumental roles.

Feminist scholarship in many fields is found in Vivian Gornick and Barbara K. Moran's *Woman in Sexist Society: Studies in Power and Powerlessness*. Among other essays, this book includes two important ones: Naomi Weisstein's "Psychology Constructs the Female" and Pauline B. Bart's "Depression in Middle-Aged Women." The first essay discusses women's psychological profile as socially constructed and enforced; the second examines the cases of middle-aged women who have lost their roles in life through divorce from or death of their spouses and the maturation of their children. Elizabeth Janeway's *Man's World, Woman's Place: A Study in Social Mythology* is an important book about the way women are defined in a patriarchal society and how the social myths perpetuated by society become self-fulfilling prophecies in women's lives.

The sociologist Jessie Bernard has written a number of influential books over the past decade on the subject of women and society. Among the more important of these are *Women and the Public Interest: An Essay on Policy and Protest, The Future of Marriage, The Future of Motherhood,* and *Women, Wives, Mothers: Values and Options.* All of these books are significant and useful because they survey so effectively recent scholarship on women's social roles, the same roles that are so rigorously reaffirmed in women's romantic fiction.

Of course, this is only a brief sample of the sociological approaches to women in modern America. New material is being published constantly and should, of course, be considered. The importance of this material, however, is that the received message of what a woman should be as defined by society parallels so closely the ways in which the heroines of woman's gothic and romantic fiction live their lives. It is probably not unreasonable to conclude that women's fiction, at least in our own day and probably long before, serves at least one purpose for its readers: that of reaffirming values that may seem to be "right" externally but may also seem "wrong" in an individual's own life. If the social pressures on women are similar, then women feeling those pressures might well converge on a form of escape entertainment that temporarily assuages those feelings of inadequacy and anxiety. Men, feeling differing pressures, would find this fiction boring and intolerable. A thorough discussion of how external socially constructed belief systems are internalized by individuals in a culture and can cause them to turn to various reality-maintenance techniques can be found in Peter L. Berger and Thomas Luckmann's *The Social Construction of Reality.*

The works cited in this chapter are merely a beginning toward defining approaches to the interpretation of popular fiction that are truly interdisciplinary. As suggested before, no work of interpretation has yet incorporated all of these approaches in a creative synthesis with literary and historical analysis. The problem remains: we must learn just how the act of reading and the prior choice of what to read relate to demography, psychological factors, sociological considerations, and aesthetic experience. This is the most significant challenge awaiting researchers into the world of women's fiction and its implications.

NOTES

1. Heinz Steinberg, "Books and Readers as a Subject of Research in Europe and America," *International Social Science Journal* 24 (1972): 745.

2. John G. Cawelti, *Adventure, Mystery, and Romance: Formula Stories As Art and Popular Culture* (Chicago: University of Chicago Press, 1976), p. 323.

3. Robert Oliphant, "Toward a Theory of Reading Sequence," *Learning Today* 6 (Summer 1973): 43-44.

4. Ibid., p. 60.

5. Robert Escarpit, *Sociology of Literature* (London: Cass, 1971), p. 88.

6. Ibid.

7. Ibid., p. 89.

8. Ibid.

9. Ibid.

10. Jan Hajda, "A Time for Reading," *Trans-Action* 4 (June 1967): 45.

11. Ibid., p. 50.

12. Yankelovich, Skelly, and White, Inc., *Consumer Research Study on Reading and Book Purchasing* (The Book Industry Study Group, Inc., October 1978), p. 18.

13. Ibid., p. 30.

14. Ibid., pp. 29-30.

15. Ibid., p. 138.

16. Ibid., p. 28.

17. Ibid., p. 71.

18. Ibid., p. 79.

19. Ibid., p. 20.

20. Ibid.

21. Ibid., p. 32.

22. Ibid.

23. Ibid., p. 143.

24. Ibid., p. 141.

25. Ibid., p. 137.

26. Ibid.

27. John Y. Cole and Carol S. Gold, eds., *Reading in America, 1978* (Washington, D.C.: Library of Congress, 1979), p. 96.

28. Peter H. Mann, *The Romantic Novel: A Survey of Reading Habits* (London: Mills and Boon, 1969), p. 3.

29. Peter H. Mann, *A New Survey: The Facts About Romantic Fiction* (London: Mills and Boon, 1974), p. 7.

30. Mann, *Romantic Novel*, p. 3.

31. Mann, *Romantic Novel*, p. 7.

32. Norman N. Holland, *The Dynamics of Literary Response* (New York: Oxford University Press, 1968), p. 66.

33. Christopher Lasch, *Haven in a Heartless World: The Family Beseiged* (New York: Basic Books, 1977), pp. 79-80.

34. Juliet Mitchell, *Psychoanalysis and Feminism* (New York: Pantheon, 1974), p. 338.

35. Phyllis Whitney, "For Personal Reference," *The Writer* 82 (February 1969): 26.

36. Erik H. Erikson, "Womanhood and the Inner Space," [1964] in *Identity: Youth and Crisis* (New York: Norton, 1968), p. 265.

37. Albert Ellis, "Romantic Love," [1962] in *Sex and Human Relationships*, ed. Cecil E. Johnson (Columbus: Charles E. Merrill, 1970), p. 31.

BIBLIOGRAPHY

Bailey, Margaret. "The Women's Magazine Short-Story Heroine in 1957 and 1967." *Journalism Quarterly* 46 (1969): 364-66.

Bardwick, Judith M. *Psychology of Women: A Study of Bio-Cultural Conflicts.* New York: Harper and Row, 1971.

_____. *Readings on the Psychology of Women.* New York: Harper and Row, 1972.

Bart, Pauline B. "Depression in Middle-Aged Women." In *Woman in Sexist Society: Studies in Power and Powerlessness,* edited by Vivian Gornick and Barbara K. Moran, pp. 99-117. New York: Basic Books, 1971.

Berger, Peter L., and Thomas Luckmann. *The Social Construction of Reality.* Garden City, N.Y.: Doubleday, Anchor, 1966.

Bernard, Jessie. *The Future of Marriage.* New York: World, 1972.

_____. *The Future of Motherhood.* New York: Dial, 1974.

_____. *Women and the Public Interest: An Essay on Policy and Protest.* Chicago: Aldine, 1971.

_____. *Women, Wives, Mothers: Values and Options.* Chicago, Aldine, 1975.

Bettelheim, Bruno. *The Uses of Enchantment: The Meaning and Importance of Fairy Tales.* New York: Alfred A. Knopf, 1976.

Bird, Caroline. *Born Female: The High Cost of Keeping Women Down.* New York: David McKay, 1968.

"Book Committee Chairman Reports Survey on Housewives' Reading." *Library Journal* 90 (15 January 1965): 212-13.

Cawelti, John G. *Adventure, Mystery, and Romance: Formula Stories As Art and Popular Culture.* Chicago: University of Chicago Press, 1976.

Cole, John Y., and Carol S. Gold, eds. *Reading in America, 1978.* Washington, D.C.: Library of Congress, 1979.

Ellis, Albert. "Romantic Love." In *Sex and Human Relationships,* edited by Cecil E. Johnson. Columbus: Charles E. Merrill, 1970. Reprinted from *The American Sexual Tragedy.* 2d ed. New York: Lyle Stuart, 1962.

Erikson, Erik H. "Womanhood and the Inner Space." In *Identity: Youth and Crisis.* New York: Norton, 1968.

Escarpit, Robert. *Sociology of Literature.* 2d ed. London: Cass, 1971.

Franzwa, Helen K. "Female Roles in Women's Magazine Fiction, 1940-1970." In *Woman: Dependent or Independent Variable?,* edited by Rhoda Kesler Unger and Florence L. Denmark. New York: Psychological Dimensions, Inc., 1975.

_____. "Working Women in Fact and Fiction." *Journal of Communication* 24 (Spring 1974): 104-9.

Freud, Sigmund. "Family Romances." In *The Sexual Enlightenment of Children.* New York: Collier Books, 1963.

_____. "The Family Romances of Neurotics." In *Collected Papers.* Vol. 5. London: Hogarth; New York: Basic Books, 1959.

Friedan, Betty. *The Feminine Mystique.* New York: Norton, 1963.

Gornick, Vivian, and Barbara K. Moran, eds. *Woman in Sexist Society: Studies in Power and Powerlessness.* New York: Basic Books, 1971.

Hajda, Jan. "A Time for Reading." *Trans-Action* 4 (June 1967): 45-50.

Hatch, Marya G., and David L. Hatch. "Problems of Married and Working Women as Presented by Three Popular Working Women's Magazines." *Social Forces* 37 (1958): 148-53.

Holland, Norman N. *The Dynamics of Literary Response.* New York: Oxford University Press, 1968.

Horney, Karen. *Feminine Psychology.* Edited by Harold Kelman. New York: Norton, 1967.

Inglis, Ruth. "An Objective Approach to the Relationship Between Fiction and Sociology." *American Sociological Review* 3 (1938): 526-33.

Janeway, Elizabeth. *Man's World, Woman's Place: A Study in Social Mythology.* New York: Dell, 1971.

Johns-Heine, Patricke, and Hans H. Gerth. "Values in Mass Periodical Fiction, 1921-1940." *Public Opinion Quarterly* 13 (Spring 1949): 105-13.

Kagan, J. "The Concept of Identification." *Psychological Review* 65 (September 1958): 296-305.

Kateley, Margaret A. "They Also Read Who Roll in Dough." *Wilson Library Bulletin* 45 (January 1971): 477-81.

Kister, K. F. "Of 'Luvs' and 'Lights.' " *Wilson Library Bulletin* 41 (January 1967): 510-13, 531.

Klein, Viola. "The Stereotype of Femininity." *Journal of Social Sciences* 6 (1950): 3-12. Reprinted in *Woman: Dependent or Independent Variable?*, edited by Rhoda Kesler Unger and Florence L. Denmark, pp. 20-30. New York: Psychological Dimensions, Inc., 1975.

Klinger, Eric. *The Structure and Functions of Fantasy.* New York: Wiley-Interscience, 1971.

Lasch, Christopher. *Haven in a Heartless World: The Family Beseiged.* New York: Basic Books, 1977.

Lipman-Blumen, Jean. "How Ideology Shapes Women's Lives." *Scientific American* 226 (January 1972): 34-42.

Mann, Margaret. *The Reading Habits of Adults: A Selected Annotated Bibliography.* London: The British Library Board, 1977.

Mann, Peter H. *Books: Buyers and Borrowers.* London: André Deutsch, 1971.

_____. *Bookselling: An Occupational Survey.* Sheffield: University of Sheffield Department of Sociological Studies, November 1971.

_____. *A New Survey: The Facts About Romantic Fiction.* London: Mills and Boon, 1974.

_____. *The Romantic Novel: A Survey of Reading Habits.* London: Mills and Boon, 1969.

_____, and Jacqueline L. Burgoyne. *Books and Reading.* London: André Deutsch, 1969.

Mead, Margaret. "Can Marriage Be For Life?" In *Sex and Human Relationships,* edited by Cecil E. Johnson. Columbus: Charles E. Merrill, 1970. Reprinted from *Male and Female: A Study of the Sexes in a Changing World.* New York: William Morrow, 1949.

Mitchell, Juliet. *Psychoanalysis and Feminism.* New York: Pantheon, 1974.

Oliphant, Robert. "Toward a Theory of Reading Sequence." *Learning Today* 6 (Summer 1973): 43-67.

Pehle, M. "Readers' Tastes as Seen by a Mobile Librarian." *Assistant Librarian* 58 (June 1965): 111-12.

Purves, Alan C., and Richard Beach. *Literature and the Reader.* Urbana, Ill.: National Council of Teachers of English, 1972.

Rubin, J. Z., F. J. Provenzano, and Z. Luria. "The Eye of the Beholder: Parents' Views on Sex of Newborns." *American Journal of Orthopsychiatry* 44 (1974): 512-19.

Sherman, Julia. *On the Psychology of Women: A Survey of Empirical Studies.* Springfield, Ill.: Charles C. Thomas, 1971.

Smith, Roger H., ed. *The American Reading Public.* New York: R. R. Bowker, 1963.

Steinberg, Heinz. "Books and Readers as a Subject of Research in Europe and America." *International Social Science Journal* 24 (1972): 744-55.

Tuchman, Gaye, Arlene Kaplan Daniels, and James Benet, eds. *Hearth and Home: Images of Women in the Mass Media.* New York: Oxford University Press, 1978.

Unger, Rhoda Kesler, and Florence L. Denmark, eds. *Woman: Dependent or Independent Variable?* New York: Psychological Dimensions, Inc., 1975.

Weisstein, Naomi. "Psychology Constructs the Female." In *Woman in Sexist Society: Studies in Power and Powerlessness,* edited by Vivian Gornick and Barbara K. Moran, pp. 133-46. New York: Basic Books, 1971.

Williams, Juanita H. *Psychology of Women: Behavior in a Biosocial Context.* 1974. Reprint. New York: Norton, 1977.

Yankelovich, Skelly, and White, Inc. *Consumer Research Study on Reading and Book Purchasing.* The Book Industry Study Group, Inc., October 1978.

CHAPTER 6

Popular Commentary on Gothic and Romantic Fiction: Journalism, Reviews, and How-to Advice

Because so few academic critics have written on gothic and romantic fiction, some of the best information about such novels is available in nonscholarly sources. Of course, these sources are rarely analytical, but they often contain material that would otherwise be unavailable. Authors of gothic and romantic fiction occasionally engage in publicity tours; sometimes newspaper reporters interview them about themselves and their work. Although book reviews of such fiction are rare, some of the major writers are regularly reviewed, and such reviews can be very informative about the books' appeal and presumed audience. The book publishing industry is necessarily interested in gothic and romantic fiction, and, at least for the past fifteen years or so, various publishing and writers' magazines have featured stories about sales figures, authors, and instructions for aspiring writers.

It is especially important, when using these materials, to consider the reliability of the source. Although the how-to articles and publishers' statements may suggest something about the limits of the formulas as perceived by practitioners, the hyperbole about quality and sales figures should be suspected. Newspaper writers and book reviewers are notably condescending toward these writers and authors, rarely taking them or their audiences as seriously as they deserve to be.

It would be impossible to mention all of the diverse sources in this category; this chapter suggests where to look and surveys impressionistically the content of the various popular sources of information over recent years. Because popular sources are not so well indexed or documented as scholarly ones, the "browsing" method often works. A few hours spent with a year's issues of *Publishers Weekly, The Writer,* or *Writer's Digest* can easily repay the time. In *Publishers Weekly,* certain departments are more fruitful than others. The advance reviews in fiction, fiction originals, and fiction reprints can be helpful. *Publishers Weekly's* fiction reviewers do very well in summarizing a book and suggesting the significance of an author. Aimed at booksellers, publishers, reviewers, and others interested in books, the magazine is, like all trade publications, more interested in boosterism than condescension. The section of the magazine called "Back to Press" can also be informative, in that it lists numbers of copies in print as subsequent editions are issued. Advertisements in the magazine, mostly aimed at booksellers but partially at reviewers, can also be useful, especially those that trumpet sales figures. The paperback bestseller lists include the top sellers around the country, week by week, on the mass market and trade lists. Sometimes, sales figures are included and occasionally there are brief descriptions of mass market or trade "candidates" that indicate a particular book will probably be on the list within a few weeks. Sometimes the business section of the magazine will have items on Harlequin or one of the other series of paperback romances, or perhaps a brief note on the latest activities of a prominent gothic or romantic writer. Marketing strategies may also be discussed in this magazine.

Another good source for browsing is the *New York Times Book Review.* Although gothic and romantic novels are rarely reviewed in those august pages, other features are consistently good sources for trends and changes in the genres. The bestseller lists in the *Times Book Review* have capsule descriptions of the novels. Letters to the editor occasionally refer to them, although this is infrequent. The three best features for information are the column called "Behind the Best Sellers," which profiles an author each week; the listing "Paperbacks: New and Noteworthy," which provides a capsule review of newly issued paperbacks; and, especially, "Paperback Talk," a column on the paperback industry, which frequently refers to events or discusses gothic and romantic fiction.

During the late 1960s and early 1970s, when the "gothic boom" was well established, a few major national publications took notice of gothic and romantic fiction through brief articles, some serious, some haughty, and some tongue-in-cheek. One of the most interesting of these was in the *New York Times Book Review,* an article by Gary Jennings called "Heathcliff Doesn't Smoke L & M's." Published in 1969, the article discusses the plight of a man trapped without reading matter except for gothic novels. With good humor, Jennings outlines the profile of the standard hero of such fiction and suggests half-seriously how these authors handle sex euphemistically. A sidebar in the same issue, "The Gothic Story" by Lewis Nichols, offers a brief summary of gothic fiction as a publishing phenomenon. Two years later, the respected *Time* book critic, Martha Duffy, discussed in her book column, subtitled that week "On the Road to Manderley," the work of four especially popular writers in the genre: Norah Lofts, Victoria Holt, Phyllis Whitney, and Mary Stewart. The article is appreciative, although not hyperbolic, taking into account the sensitivity of both the authors and the audience to criticism about the seriousness of their intentions. This article was important because it revealed in a mass circulation magazine the identity of Victoria Holt. Through much of the decade of the 1960s, speculation about the author behind the pseudonym had grown—some even suggested she was Daphne du Maurier—although her identity was noted, for example, in Ordean A. Hagen's *Who Done It?*, a reference work on mystery and detective fiction. Holt is Eleanor Burford Hibbert, whose work was familiar to some readers through her historical romance series written under the name Jean Plaidy. Shortly after Duffy's article, Hibbert's publisher went public and hailed a new series of "historical gothics" by Hibbert writing under the name Philippa Carr. As for the other authors mentioned by Duffy, it is noteworthy that only one of them was American, Phyllis Whitney, a writer of gothics and juvenile mysteries. Of the others, Mary Stewart had given up the writing of gothics several years before in order to turn to her now-completed trilogy of historical novels about Merlin and King Arthur, while Norah Lofts was a prolific and established writer of historical romances. (As an indication of the blurred outlines between the various women's romantic formulas, it is interesting that Lofts, writing under a pseudonym in 1978, won a British publisher's competition for writing a novel in the mode of Georgette Heyer, who died in 1974. Heyer was the mistress of the Regency Romance; Lofts's imitation was published as *The Day of the Butterfly* [1979], a book distributed in this country by the Doubleday Book Club, probably the major book club featuring women's fiction.)

Two earlier and similar articles on the gothic phenomenon were "Heathcliff, Cliff-Hangers" in *Newsweek* and "Extricating Emily" in *Time*, both published in 1966. In the past several years, both news magazines have had articles on the new "erotic gothic" trends. Mass market magazines have also profiled authors from earlier years. In 1919, the *Saturday Evening Post* ran a brief article on Temple Bailey, a fairly obscure but interesting romantic writer. *Life* published a chatty biography of Mary Roberts Rinehart by Geoffrey T. Hellman in 1946. Margaret Mitchell has had much attention in magazines, including a 1962 version of her life by A. D. Edwards in the *Reader's Digest* series "My Most Unforgettable Character." M. F. Perkerson's "Mystery of Margaret Mitchell" in *Look* in 1955 is a discussion of the rumors about her and the destruction of the manuscript of *Gone With the Wind*. An *American Mercury* profile, A. S. Harris's "Scarlett Gave Her a Pot of Gold," is especially informative. Other useful journalistic sources include: A. Cordell's "Strange Story Behind *Gone With the Wind*," in *Coronet* in 1961; Fletcher Knebel's "Scarlett O'Hara's Millions," in *Look* in 1963; "First of the Month," in *Saturday Review* in 1967; and "*GWTW*'s Start," an excerpt from Margaret Mitchell's letters in 1976 in *Vogue*. These are, of course, only posthumous articles about her, indicating the continuing interest in the author and her novel. The magazines of the 1930s abounded in articles on her.

Daphne du Maurier has been similarly fascinating to editors of mass market magazines. Interviews or profiles have appeared in *Ladies' Home Journal* in 1956, by B. Nichols; in *Saturday Review* in 1957, by Oliver K. Whiting; and in *Ladies' Home Journal* in 1971, anonymously written and entitled "Romantic." An excerpt from her autobiography, *Myself When Young*, appeared in the *Saturday Evening Post* in 1977. In addition to the spate of publicity that surrounded Kathleen Winsor after the publication of *Forever Amber* in 1944, her later books also aroused some interest, although she seems to have left the gothic/romance field to others after that successful novel. A *Look* article in 1954, P. Coffin's "Kay Winsor Launches a New Career," discussed her life and her work. Reviews of later works can be found in *Time* in 1957 in the "Books" column, and in *Newsweek* in 1965 (see Winsor in bibliography), the latter including Winsor's reactions to negative reviews of *Wanderers Eastward, Wanderers West* (1965). Daphne du Maurier, Margaret Mitchell, and Kathleen Winsor in a period of about eight years wrote three of the major works of gothic and romantic fiction in this century. None followed the first book with another of the type, although du Maurier and Winsor are still writing. Mitchell, of course, wrote only one novel before her death. Both du Maurier and Winsor defined a standard for their particular version of the genre, never equalled their own best work, but inspired countless other writers who were to come. Significantly, the only du Maurier book that is constantly mentioned in articles and reviews about gothic novels is *Rebecca*, and *Forever Amber* is the book against which all of Winsor's later novels have been judged.

Another writer who produced one fine example of romantic fiction and then went on to other kinds of writing is Marcia Davenport, whose 1942 novel, *Valley of Decision*, has been exceptionally popular among women readers for almost forty years. The novel was made into a film shortly after its release; it is typical of the genre we would today call the "family saga," similar to books written recently by Susan Howatch. Set in the steel mills of Pennsylvania, the book is the love story of the patrician son and the Irish servant of a steel magnate kept perpetually apart by social distinction and pride. A chatty, but informative, biography of Marcia Davenport, by J. Whitbread, is found in *Good Housekeeping* in 1960. She, too, continued to write but never ventured fully into the romantic field after *Valley of Decision*.

One of the finest American writers of historical romances is Anya Seton, who, unlike so many other gothic and romantic writers, has written relatively few books. Her first, *Dragonwyck* (1944), was a gothic novel, later filmed, but all of her subsequent books have been massive historical novels about women. Interest in Seton sometimes is more intense than usual for such books because of her meticulous historical research, and she has occasionally been discussed in slightly more serious terms than some other writers. When *Ladies' Home Journal* excerpted her book *Katherine* in 1954, it included a brief informative introduction. *Scholastic* magazine, in an anonymous article entitled "Cavalcade Books," discussed her for a high school audience in 1955. A biographical sketch by Rollene Waterman that includes information about her research for *The Winthrop Woman*, the number twelve book on Hackett's all-time bestseller list, appeared in *Saturday Review* in 1958. The *New Yorker* featured her in 1962 in its "Talk of the Town" column.

Journalistic material on Georgette Heyer is infrequent, although the *New York Times* published a long and detailed obituary when she died in 1974. The best information on her, in addition to the obituary, is her husband's (G. R. Rougier's) preface to an edition of her unfinished novel, *My Lord John*, published in 1975. A brief biography of Mary Stewart by A. H. Horowitz appeared in the *Wilson Library Bulletin* in 1960; however, a much more interesting piece on her is F. W. J. Hemmings's article in *New Statesman* in which he appreciatively analyzes her fiction. She was interviewed, along with a large number of other writers, for Roy Newquist's book, *Counterpoint*; the interview is detailed and constitutes the best statement of Stewart's intentions and writing philosophy. Because Mary Stewart's books are adventurous enough to attract the attention of some male mystery buffs, she has also attracted more attention from reviewers than most of her colleagues. For example, Anthony Boucher regularly reviewed her early work in his column on mystery fiction for the *New York Times*. Norah Lofts is profiled in *Saturday Review*, in 1954 by Sara Henderson Hay and in 1955 by Oliver LaFarge.

The journalists' favorite writer in recent years has been Barbara Cartland, who seeks publicity for herself as well as for her work. Cartland is British, loosely connected to the upper classes, and an unabashed spokesperson for a variety of conservative and out-of-the-mainstream causes, such as royalty, jewelry, health food, chastity, and romance. Sources on her are numerous in magazines, including her mother's reminiscences in *Listener* in 1973, "My Wonderful Daughter— Polly Cartland Talks to John Pitman about Barbara." *Saturday Evening Post* featured her as the "Queen of Romance" in 1978, by K. Munro. *MacLeans* featured her "One-Woman Library of Love" by A. F. Gonzalez in 1978. A magazine called *50 Plus* profiled her in 1979 in A. F. Gonzalez's "Barbara Cartland: Mistress of the Fiction Factory." And the *New York Times Book Review* announced her upcoming American tour in 1979. During that tour, she was interviewed by Judy Bachrach of the *Washington Star*, whose article, "Barbara Cartland, Virginity for Fun and Lots of Profit," contains Cartland at her quintessential best. The picture that accompanies the article shows Cartland's outrageous personal image, as found on the covers of most of her books: fluffy white hair, dressed in flowing gown and too much jewelry, and accompanied by her ever-present white dog. An even better Cartland interview, with Mike Wallace, was aired on CBS-TV's *Sixty Minutes* in 1977. A transcript was available from CBS shortly after the interview. Every time Cartland tours America, she can be heard on talk shows.

Recently, some journalists have turned their attention to the Harlequin Romances phenomenon. A story about the organization appeared in the "Advertising" column by Philip H. Dougherty in the *New York Times* in early 1980. In 1979, when Harlequin threw a thank-you birthday party for faithful readers in the Washington, D.C., area, both of the local papers covered the party and interviewed readers. Each of those articles, by Judy Bachrach in the *Washington Star* and Lynn Darling in the *Washington Post*, is a good example of the typical newspaper attitude toward such fiction: condescending, slightly contemptuous, yet recognizing (while holding the nose) that readers care. Another journalistic article was unusual: at a session at the 1979 American Studies Association meeting, John Cawelti, Kay Mussell, Ann Douglas, and Mary Lynn discussed the phenomenon of pulp romantic fiction and its relationship to male pornography. The session was covered for the *St. Paul Sunday Pioneer Press* by Carole Nelson, herself a writer of gothic novels. As a popular interpretation of critical opinion on women's romantic fiction, the article is interesting and valuable. In 1977, the *Washington Post Book World* featured a special section on paperbacks. Carol Rinzler's contribution, "Gush!," is a reasonable, only slightly condescending, discussion of paperback fiction appealing to women.

The best source for the few reviews of individual books that are available is *Book Review Digest*, although *Book Review Index* is occasionally helpful. *Book Review Digest* has the advantage of including short excerpts from many of the reviews, and it also notes the number of words so that a researcher can decide whether the review is long or thorough enough to merit attention. This is particularly important in the case of reviews in newspapers since, with the exception of a few major papers, back issues are available only on microfilm, if at all. Occasionally, a newspaper or magazine will commission an essay-review on several gothic or romantic novels; these are usually more serious and more useful than reviews of individual books. Most notable among these is Michele Murray's essay-review, "Genteel Escape Literature," in the *Washington Post*, in which she evaluates sympathetically the appeal of women's fiction in terms of its presumed audience. Her comments on the powerlessness of women and the need for escape through fiction that portrays women in exciting situations are sensitive and sure.

Another nonscholarly article of some interest is Regina Minudri's "From Jane to Germaine, With Love," a librarian's somewhat simplistic analysis of why gothic novels are popular. She suggests that gothic heroines are prototypes of liberated women, an idea that seems reasonable on the surface but that ignores the much more complex relationship between heroines and their readers.

Since some authors have made millions writing gothic and romantic novels, although many others have failed or barely made ends meet, the how-to-do-it field is a rich one, dominated by articles in *The Writer*. This material is especially valuable because it reveals several otherwise unnoticed aspects of the fiction in recent years. It shows unequivocally the seriousness with which authors approach their work. The most successful authors do not see themselves as genre writers and resent being categorized neatly into pejorative slots. They work hard and are probably more reflective about what it is they are doing than most of their publishers. They believe that their success can be duplicated and they are clearly conscious of the formula within which they write, but they do not see it as less worthy of notice than other kinds of fiction. They do not condescend to their audience.

Two book-length how-to-do-it volumes are from British publishers.

Anne Britton and Marion Collin's *Romantic Fiction* is a book of advice to would-be authors of women's romances. Among other things, they caution writers to take the fiction as seriously as the readers do, suggesting that condescension is the surest road to failure. A similar book, Claire Ritchie's *Writing the Romantic Novel*, is another handbook for aspiring writers. It is a very practical approach with little definition of the genre. The American writer, Phyllis Whitney, also wrote a how-to-do-it book, *Writing Juvenile Stories and Novels*, a very thoughtful book with practical and philosophical advice. The information in this book, telling us how she constructs and revises a plot, illuminates the Phyllis Whitney material at the Boston University Library, described in Appendix 1.

General advice essays to would-be writers have appeared in both *The Writer* and *Writer's Digest* with some regularity over the past several years. A particularly informative one is Janet Louise Roberts's "Writing and Selling the Gothic Novel," in *Writer's Digest*, an essay that contains a good basic history of the genre along with a discussion of publishing houses and the economics of writing such fiction. Standard how-to articles in *The Writer* include Elsie Lee's "When You Write a Gothic" and Elizabeth Peters's "Character and Humor in Gothics." One of the most popular forms of romantic fiction in the late seventies has been the family saga, tracing one family's experiences through several generations, innumerable pages, and sometimes several volumes. D. K. Hall's "Writing the Romantic Saga" discusses how writers might break into that field.

Some of the major writers of gothic and romantic fiction have also written in these publications; the most prolific writer is Phyllis Whitney. Two of the most interesting articles, however, are by the author who is probably the best craftsperson in the field, Mary Stewart. In *The Writer* in 1964, Stewart's essay, "Setting and Background in the Novel," reveals Stewart's intense concern with setting and with description, at which she is expert. Most commentators on her work have praised her careful delineation of setting and have showed how she integrates it well with plot and characters. She is particularly proud of what she calls the "organic use of setting" and shows in this essay how she likes to work. In 1970, she wrote for the magazine again; this time her title was "Teller of Tales." Stewart, more than most romantic writers, likes to think of herself as a storyteller without limitation by constraints of formula. In this essay, she sets out her credo.

Another careful writer, Anya Seton, has also written two essays for *The Writer*. The first, "Treasure Hunt of Research," is a meticulous account of how she does her prodigious research for each novel. Seton is probably the best "historian" among writers of historical romances. Rather than merely providing period details as backgrounds for romantic plots, she carefully reads the original sources and takes scholarly controversy into account before she begins writing. She visits the settings of her books before she writes about them. Unlike such writers as Georgette Heyer, she does not make one historical period her own and use it for book after book. Instead, she chooses a different location and time for each book and does her own research into the subject, using, for example, fourteenth-century England for one novel, eighteenth-century England and America for another, and seventeenth-century Massachusetts for a third. She also uses original documents, learning to read Middle English and Middle French for *Katherine* (1954), and obtaining and using her own multivolume set of the Winthrop Papers for *The Winthrop Woman* (1958). Although she feels free to invent motivation and character after she knows her subject, her books have an authentic "feel" unusual in woman's romances. This article tells how she does it. The second, "Writer's Requisites," is an essay about the craft of writing and Seton's own habits in setting words down on paper and revising them.

Phyllis Whitney is almost a fixture in the pages of *The Writer*, although she occasionally writes advice articles for other publications. Some of these pieces must surely be derived from her numerous writing workshops and classes on writing. In 1954, she wrote an essay entitled "Plus Factor," outlining the differences between a mediocre and a successful writer. Among her items of counsel are the necessity of writing about familiar topics, the need to consider problems that affect many people rather than just a few, and the necessity of having a message that can be conveyed subtly. A 1961 essay, "Know-how and Experience," says that in order to learn how to write a book you must simply do it. "Writing the Juvenile Mystery" tells how she chooses titles, develops characters, and decides on subjects. Whitney for years has been writing one gothic romance and one juvenile mystery each year. In 1965, in "Satisfying Element," Whitney states that emotion is important in fiction. The writer cannot name feelings but must use sensory details and emotional reactions of the characters to be effective. She says she tries to act out in her mind the scene she will write about on any given day. "Map Is Not a Journey" details how she plans her writing to produce two books a year. Her most important *Writer* article came in 1967. Entitled "Writing the Gothic Novel," the essay delineates Whitney's ideas on the form and includes her judgments on writers who try to exploit the formula—she is especially harsh on male writers who write under female pseudonyms—and some of her own personal likes and dislikes in the field. "For Personal Reference" is a listing of the books she keeps in her personal library to help her write. "Where It Happens: Backgrounds for Fiction" is a discussion of how she develops setting, often travelling to the site but sometimes doing extensive research instead. "I Couldn't Put It Down" is a discussion of what makes a good novel. "Opportunity Is Like a Train" offers advice to writers on what to do when they cannot publish their work. She says that she worked as a reviewer and conducted writing seminars. After she perfected her writing, the opportunity to publish came along. This is a good history of her writing career. "Springboard to Fiction" is an article on what to do when the ideas run dry. "Leaving the Reader Satisfied" discusses the problem of providing growth and change in a character so that the reader is satisfied that the character's fate in the ending was deserved. "Using the Force" also offers advice to would-be writers.

Norah Lofts is another popular writer whose self-consciousness about her work has led to a number of advice articles in *Writer*. Her 1960 article, "On Writing Historical Fiction," discusses her technique of looking for similarities between past and present characters in order to provide a link between reader and character. She uses modern language rather than attempting dialect, uses relatively little costume description, and tries to avoid writing about historically controversial issues. "Finding the Straw for the Bricks" discusses how she does her research. "Throw Your Heart Over" is an essay on how to provide imagination in a novel and to help the reader escape. "Ticket to Timbuktu: Writing About Unfamiliar Places" tells how to use research to substitute for on-site visits in creating setting. "Getting To Know Them" uses one of her characters as an example of how to get inside a character to create realism. In "Choosing an Historical Character," Lofts advises writers to choose a character with human weaknesses and faults who is interesting enough to "live with" while writing the book. "What Makes a Good Story?" suggests that writers must have a sense of direction. They should eschew coincidence and use many details, such as how the characters support themselves and how they live. "Random Thoughts on Fiction Writing" asserts that the novel is a form of escapism. Characters and situations, however, must be presented realistically; style and pace must move quickly. She says a writer is never lonely.

A few other authors have also offered advice in the pages of *The Writer*. Daoma Winston, a fairly competent writer of historical novels usually set in America, wrote an essay in 1978 entitled "Historical Romances." Dorothy Eden's 1972 essay, "Elusive Plot," discusses how she lets her plots evolve through her characters' development. Susan Howatch's "Road to a Best Seller" is especially interesting in its description of how she prepared to write *Penmarric* (1971). In three "big" books of the 1970s, Howatch did historical research and then transplanted her romantic story to a modern era. *Penmarric* tells the tale of Henry II, Eleanor of Acquitaine, and the Fair Rosamund but places it not in twelfth-century England but in nineteenth-century Cornwall. In "Realism in Modern Gothics," Howatch says that meticulous, suspenseful plotting is essential. Characters must have depth and there must be an interesting but not overwhelming setting. Writing about *Penmarric* and *Cashelmara* (1974), her retelling of the story of three British kings—Edward I, II, and III—and their families, Howatch describes in "Risks and Rewards in Writing the Saga Novel" how she provides coherence and development in a sprawling story. *Cashelmara* moves the story from fourteenth-century England to nineteenth-century Ireland. The third book in which she used this technique is *The Rich Are Different* (1977), a version of the Julius Caesar, Cleopatra, and Marc Antony triangle set in twentieth-century England and America. A much earlier advice essay, in 1955 by Susan Sibley, is "Accent on Love: Writing for Women's Magazines," in which the author tells writers how to handle love stories in short fiction.

A few other off-beat articles might also be consulted, although these are not the most useful analytic pieces available. In 1925 and 1927, Irving Harlow Hart surveyed bestsellers and popular authors since 1895 in four articles for *Publishers Weekly*. An author-student panel is reported by G. L. Jones in *Library Journal* in 1960, referring to an appearance by Phyllis Whitney before a group of students. An article in *English Journal* by R. P. Hildebrand recommends Anya Seton's *Katherine* as a good book for high school English teachers to use in their classes because it explains the history and the social and moral order of medieval England in a form comprehensible to teenagers. An article in *Publishers Weekly* in 1971 discusses Lolah Burford, the author of several recent "erotic gothics." "Story Behind the Book, *Vice Avenged, A Moral Tale*" by B. A. B. tells how indebted Burford is to Georgette Heyer and how she was able to place her book with a publisher. It also outlines her future plans as a writer.

Theoretical and analytical discussion of gothic and romantic fiction is not advanced by using these journalistic and publishing sources, but researchers should survey this material with care for it often is the raw data that is needed to support analysis of individual novels and authors. Unsystematic, sketchy, hyperbolic, condescending, or self-congratulatory it may be; but it is fitting that an ephemeral entertainment such as women's romantic fiction should be best chronicled and catalogued in ephemeral sources. This adds to the problems of research; but it also adds to the fun.

BIBLIOGRAPHY

B. A. B. "The Story Behind the Book: *Vice Avenged, A Moral Tale."* *Publishers Weekly* 200 (12 July 1971): 52-53.

Bachrach, Judy. "Barbara Cartland, Virginity for Fun and Lots of Proft." *Washington Star*, 17 July 1979, pp. D1-2.

_____. "A Romantic Publisher Hits 30." *Washington Star*, 19 October 1979, pp. D10-11.

"Books." Review of *America, With Love*, by Kathleen Winsor. *Time* 70 (14 October 1957): 122.

Britton, Anne, and Marion Collin. *Romantic Fiction.* London: T. V. Boardman, 1960.

"Cavalcade Books." *Scholastic* 67 (22 September 1955): 32T.

Coffin, P. "Kay Winsor Launches a New Career." *Look* 18 (10 August 1954): 70.

Cordell, A. "Strange Story Behind *Gone With the Wind." Coronet* 48 (February 1961): 98-104.

Darling, Lynn. "Harlequin Presents . . . A World of Romance with a Happy Ending." *Washington Post*, 19 October 1979, pp. B1, B7.

Dougherty, Philip H. "Selling Books Like Tide." *New York Times*, 26 February 1980.

Duffy, Martha. "On the Road to Manderley." *Time* 97 (12 April 1971): 95-96.

du Maurier, Daphne. "Place Has Taken Hold of Me: Menabilly." Excerpt from *Myself When Young. Saturday Evening Post* 249 (December 1977): 48-50.

Eden, Dorothy. "Elusive Plot." *The Writer* 85 (December 1972): 9-10.

Edwards, A. D. "My Most Unforgettable Character: Margaret Mitchell." *Reader's Digest* 80 (March 1962): 117-21.

"Extricating Emily." *Time* 87 (11 April 1966): 88.

"First of the Month: Margaret Mitchell." *Saturday Review* 50 (5 August 1967): 2.

Gonzalez, A. F. "Barbara Cartland: Mistress of the Fiction Factory." *50 Plus* 19 (April 1979): 40-41.

_____. "One-Woman Library of Love." *MacLeans* 91 (11 December 1978): 14.

Hagen, Ordean A. *Who Done It? A Guide to Detective, Mystery, and Suspense Fiction.* New York: R. R. Bowker, 1969.

Hall, D. K. "Writing the Romantic Saga." *The Writer* 91 (August 1978): 13-15.

Harris, A. S. "Scarlett Gave Her a Pot of Gold." *American Mercury* 86 (February 1958): 136-43.

Hart, Irving Harlow. "Best Sellers in Fiction During the First Quarter of the Twentieth Century." *Publishers Weekly* 107 (14 February 1925): 525-27.

_____. "Fiction Fashions from 1895 to 1926." *Publishers Weekly* 111 (5 February 1927): 473-77.

_____. "The Most Popular Authors of Fiction Between 1900 and 1925." *Publishers Weekly* 107 (21 February 1925): 619-22.

_____. "The Most Popular Authors of Fiction in the Post-War Period, 1919-1926." *Publishers Weekly* 111 (12 March 1927): 1045-53.

Hay, Sara Henderson. "A Suffolk State." Review of *Bless This House,* by Norah Lofts. *Saturday Review* 37 (27 March 1954): 16-17.

"Heathcliff, Cliff-Hangers." *Newsweek* 67 (4 April 1966): 101-2.

Hellman, Geoffrey T. "Mary Roberts Rinehart." *Life* 20 (25 February 1946): 55-56, 58, 61-62.

Hemmings, F. W. J. "Mary Queen of Hearts." *New Statesman* 70 (5 November 1965): 698-99.

"Heyer, Georgette." Obituary. *New York Times,* July 1974.

Hildebrand, R. P. "*Katherine* by Anya Seton for High School Seniors." *English Journal* 60 (September 1971): 746-47.

Horowitz, A. H. "WLB Biography: Mary Stewart." *Wilson Library Bulletin* 35 (December 1960): 328.

Howatch, Susan. "Realism in Modern Gothics." *The Writer* 87 (May 1974): 11-13.

_____. "Risks and Rewards in Writing the Saga Novel." *The Writer* 90 (June 1977): 11-13.

_____. "Road to a Best Seller." *The Writer* 84 (December 1971): 11-12.

Jennings, Gary. "Heathcliff Doesn't Smoke L & M's." *New York Times Book Review,* 27 July 1969.

Jones, G. L. "Author-Student Panel: Phyllis Whitney." *Library Journal* 85 (15 January 1960): 327.

Knebel, Fletcher. "Scarlett O'Hara's Millions." *Look* 27 (3 December 1963): 39-40.

LaFarge, Oliver. "Westward Horror." Review of *Winter Harvest,* by Norah Lofts. *Saturday Review* 38 (19 November 1955): 21.

Lambert, Gavin. "The Making of *Gone With the Wind.*" 2 parts. *Atlantic* 231 (February 1973): 37-51: (March 1973): 56-72. Part II with comment on the movie by Andrew Sarris, Stanley Kauffman, Judith Crist, Arthur Schlesinger, Jr., and Richard Schickel.

Lee, Elsie. "When You Write a Gothic." *The Writer* 86 (May 1973): 17-19, 35.

Lofts, Norah. "Choosing an Historical Character." *The Writer* 85 (December 1972): 21-22.

_____. "Finding the Straw for the Bricks." *The Writer* 75 (July 1962): 17-19.

_____. "Getting to Know Them." *The Writer* 83 (November 1970): 9-10.

_____. "On Writing Historical Fiction." *The Writer* 73 (May 1960): 10-11.

_____. "Random Thoughts on Fiction Writing." *The Writer* 89 (July 1976): 12-14.

_____. "Throw Your Heart Over." *The Writer* 78 (December 1965): 11-13.

_____. "Ticket to Timbuktu: Writing About Unfamiliar Places." *The Writer* 80 (June 1967): 11-13.

_____. "What Makes a Good Story?" *The Writer* 87 (March 1974): 11-12.

Minudri, Regina. "From Jane to Germaine, With Love." *Library Journal* 98 (15 February 1973): 658-59.

Mitchell, Margaret. *"GWTW*'s Start: Excerpts from *Margaret Mitchell's "Gone With the Wind" Letters.*" *Vogue* 166 (September 1976): 350-51, 376-79.

Munro, K. "Queen of Romance." *Saturday Evening Post* 250 (March 1978): 58-59.

Murray, Michele. "Genteel Escape Literature." *Washington Post Book World,* 18 February 1973, p. 3.

Nelson, Carole. "Romance, Pornography: Entwined But Not Linked." *St. Paul Sunday Pioneer Press,* 7 October 1979, p. 2.

Newquist, Roy. *Counterpoint.* Chicago: Rand-McNally, 1964.

Nichols, B. "Daphne du Maurier." *Ladies' Home Journal* 73 (November 1956): 25.

Nichols, Lewis. "The Gothic Story." *New York Times Book Review,* 27 July 1969, p. 25.

Perkerson, M. F. "Mystery of Margaret Mitchell." *Look* 19 (15 November 1955): 113-16.

Peters, Elizabeth. "Character and Humor in Gothics." *The Writer* 89 (November 1976): 15-17.

Pitman, John. "My Wonderful Daughter—Polly Cartland Talks to John Pitman About Barbara." *Listener* 89 (22 March 1973): 375-76.

Rinzler, Carol. "Gush!" *Washington Post Book World,* 13 March 1977, pp. E1-2.

Ritchie, Claire. *Writing the Romantic Novel.* London: Bond St. Publishers, 1962.

Roberts, Janet Louise. "Writing and Selling the Gothic Novel." *Writer's Digest* 53 (January 1973): 25-27.

"Romantic." *Ladies' Home Journal* 88 (August 1971): 102.

Rougier, G. R. Preface to *My Lord John,* by Georgette Heyer. New York: E. P. Dutton, 1975.

Seton, Anya. Excerpt from *"Katherine." Ladies' Home Journal* 71 (June 1954): 3.

_____. "Treasure Hunt of Research." *The Writer* 75 (April 1962): 33.

_____. "Writer's Requisites." *The Writer* 80 (August 1967): 19.

Sibley, Susan. "Accent on Love: Writing for Women's Magazines." *The Writer* 68 (February 1955): 45-47.

Stewart, Mary. "Setting and Background in the Novel." *The Writer* 77 (December 1964): 7-9.

_____. "Teller of Tales." *The Writer* 83 (May 1970): 9-12.

"Take Me Back to Manderley." Review of *The Scapegoat,* by Daphne du Maurier. *Time* 69 (25 February 1957): 102.

"Talk of the Town: Best Seller (Anya Seton)." *New Yorker* 38 (12 May 1962): 34.

"Temple Bailey." *Saturday Evening Post* 192 (15 November 1919): 49.

Wallace, Mike. "Queen of Hearts." Interview with Barbara Cartland. *Sixty Minutes,* CBS-TV, 3 April 1977.

Walters, Ray. "Paperback Talk." *New York Times Book Review* 84 (4 March 1979): 41.

Waterman, Rollene. "The Author (Anya Seton)." *Saturday Review* 41 (15 February 1958): 20.

Whitbread, J. "The Remarkable Marcia Davenport." *Good Housekeeping,* April 1960, pp. 26-28.

Whiting, Oliver K. "A Visit With Daphne du Maurier." *Saturday Review* 40 (23 February 1957): 16-17.

Whitney, Phyllis. "For Personal Reference." *The Writer* 82 (February 1969): 23-26.

_____. "I Couldn't Put It Down." *The Writer* 86 (April 1973): 11-14, 23.

_____. "Know-how and Experience." *The Writer* 74 (November 1961): 24.

_____. "Leaving the Reader Satisfied." *The Writer* 90 (April 1977): 13-16.

_____. "Map Is Not a Journey." *The Writer* 78 (November 1965): 7-12.

_____. "Opportunity Is Like a Train." *The Writer* 87 (November 1974): 11-13.

_____. "Plus Factor." *The Writer* 67 (April 1954): 116-19.

_____. "Satisfying Element." *The Writer* 78 (February 1965): 11-14.

_____. "Springboard to Fiction." *The Writer* 89 (October 1976): 11-15.

_____. "Using the Force." *The Writer* 92 (January 1979): 11-15.

_____. "Where It Happens: Backgrounds for Fiction." *The Writer* 85 (January 1972): 14-15.

_____. "Writing the Gothic Novel." *The Writer* 80 (February 1967): 9-13, 42-43.

_____. "Writing the Juvenile Mystery." *The Writer* 76 (April 1963): 14-18.

_____. *Writing Juvenile Stories and Novels.* Boston: The Writer, 1976.

Winsor, Kathleen. Interview. "Books: 11,623 Hours." *Newsweek* 65 (24 May 1965): 114.

Winston, Daoma. "Historical Romances." *The Writer* 91 (November 1978): 11-14.

PERIODICALS

Book Review Digest. New York: H. W. Wilson, 1905-.

Book Review Index. Detroit: Gale Research, 1965-.

New York Times Book Review (title varies). New York: *New York Times,* 1896-.

Publishers Weekly. New York: R. R. Bowker, 1872.

The Writer. Boston: The Writer, Inc., 1887-.

Writer's Digest. Cincinnati: Atlas, 1920-.

Collections
and Research
Facilities

Gothic and romantic fiction are found in great profusion in research collections in the United States, although they are rarely catalogued under those designations. Because the rise of fiction in America coincided with the peak of influence of the gothic on popular fiction, many collections of early American fiction are fruitful sources for the researcher. The Lee Ash and Denis Lorenz guides to subject collections, described in Chapter 2, list major collections of early American fiction at the American Antiquarian Society, New York University, the Athenaeum of Philadelphia, and the University of Pittsburgh, which has the Hervey Allen Collection of two thousand volumes and related manuscripts in American historical fiction. The most extensive collection of books and manuscripts, especially for the early period, is the New York Public Library. Many libraries, including the Library of Congress, have volumes listed in Lyle H. Wright's bibliographies of early American fiction, described in Chapter 2; efforts to publish many of the volumes on microfiche continue.

Dime novel and paperback fiction collections in various libraries are also good sources for gothic and romantic novels, although these collections are often uncatalogued. For example, the Library of Congress's collection of dime novels includes twenty thousand volumes, but they are indexed only by the name of the series in which they were published in the nineteenth century. However, many of the series deposited there contain gothic and romantic novels by such authors as "Bertha M. Clay," E. D. E. N. Southworth, and other major formula writers for women in the nineteenth century. Volumes from Street and Smith's Bertha M. Clay Library are there. Ash lists other collections of dime novels at the University of California at Los Angeles, Yale University, the New York Public Library, and New York University. Northern Illinois

University at De Kalb has the Albert Johannsen Collection of eleven hundred
catalogued volumes and some related materials; the University of Alberta,
Canada, has a collection that is especially strong in "penny dreadfuls" and
gothics. Both Oberlin College and the Cleveland Public Library have collections;
Cleveland is especially strong in nineteenth-century romances. Charles Bragin
in *Bibliography: Dime Novels, 1860-1964* lists his own collection as the largest
private one (1525 W. 12th St., Brooklyn, N.Y.) and adds the University of
Minnesota collection.

Major collections of gothic novels, although not mainly American, include
the Sadleir-Black Gothic Collection at the University of Virginia (two thousand
volumes), described in Robert Kerr Black's *The Sadleir-Black Gothic Collection*;
the Yale University Library; and the University of California at Los Angeles
(three hundred). One other library collection of interest is the Barnard College
Library collection of manuscripts and books by American women authors. The
collection, contributed by Bertha Van Riper Overbury, contains nearly
two thousand books, mostly rare, written by American women, along with
almost one thousand manuscripts. The New York Public Library also contains
catalogues of lending libraries and booksellers in the eighteenth and nineteenth
centuries.

The Library of Congress's Manuscript Division contains the Ernest E. Leisy
Collection on the American Historical Novel. The collection contains manuscripts
and related material from about 1923 to 1950 and includes 450 items relating
to his research for his published study, *The American Historical Novel*. Elmira
College in Elmira, New York, has a 100-volume catalogued collection entitled
"Genteel Women's Reading, 1855-1955." In Portland, Maine, the Westbrook College Library has a collection of twelve hundred volumes written by Maine women
writers. The collection is especially noteworthy for some rare editions of novels by
Madame Wood, one of the earliest American writers of romantic and gothic fiction.

Because so much fiction of the nineteenth century was serialized, another
valuable, although uncatalogued, source is nineteenth-century newspapers and
story papers. E. D. E. N. Southworth, for example, wrote for the *New York
Ledger*, the *National Era*, the *Saturday Evening Post*, the *New York Weekly* (Street
and Smith), and the *Baltimore Saturday Visiter*. Mary Noel's book, *Villains Galore*,
mentions and describes many of the nineteenth-century story papers that a
researcher might wish to locate.

The three major institutional libraries in the United States for a researcher in
this field are the Library of Congress, the New York Public Library, and
the Boston University Library. Each has different strengths based upon distinct
functions and collecting strategies and imperatives. As the United States copyright
depository, the Library of Congress collection of fiction is excellent, especially
in the Rare Book Room. Finding romantic novels in the Library of Congress,
either in the general collection or in the Rare Book Room, is a hit or
miss process but it repays the work. In the general collection, fiction is
catalogued in categories PZ3 and PZ4, the call number referring to the author.
Without the name of an author, other strategies must be employed. The finder's
guide in the Rare Book Room lists dime novels only by series title, but some

of those titles are descriptive and will aid in the location of books and authors. The wealth of the collection at the Library of Congress derives from its eclectic nature. In many cases, fairly complete hardbound collections of a particular author's works exist virtually untouched on the shelves. If an author who wrote romantic and gothic fiction in the twentieth century can be identified, chances are that the works published in hard covers will be available. The Rare Book Room's collection, of course, is not so comprehensive, but it is a fine one. Researchers should begin by consulting the R. Glenn Wright multivolume *Bibliography*, described in Chapter 2.

The New York Public Library has several collections that include popular fiction. The Berg Collection of English and American Literature is excellent. The collection includes material on Amelia Edith Barr, Lydia Maria Child, Maria Susanna Cummins, Edna Ferber, Fannie Hurst, Helen Hunt Jackson, Mary Johnston, Kathleen Norris, Mary Roberts Rinehart, Catharine Maria Sedgwick, Lydia Huntley Sigourney, Harriet Prescott Spofford, and Jean Webster. Much of this material is from the files of the American Play Company and relates to dramatic adaptations of those author's novels.

The New York Public Library's Manuscripts and Archives Division is even more helpful than the Berg Collection. The collections relating to the careers of the nineteenth-century literary men Evert A. Duyckinck and George L. Duyckinck are particularly rich. As editors of *Arcturus, Literary World,* and the *Cyclopedia of American Literature,* the Duyckincks had correspondence with a wide variety of writers in their time. The correspondence is catalogued alphabetically by correspondent. Writers included are Caroline Chesebrough, Lydia Maria Child, Caroline Howard Gilman (whose delightful letter to a friend about her math anxiety makes her sound very modern indeed), Caroline Kirkland, Maria J. McIntosh, Susanna Haswell Rowson, Catharine Maria Sedgwick, Lydia Sigourney, Elizabeth Oakes Smith, E. D. E. N. Southworth, Tabitha Tenny, and Susan Bogert Warner. Also in that division is the Macmillan Collection, described in Chapter 2.

The Rare Book Collection at the New York Public Library has the Beadle Collection of Dime Novels, the gift of Dr. Frank P. O'Brien (fourteen hundred volumes), and a chapbook file. The Arents Collection of Books in Parts (including serials, "shilling shockers," and "penny dreadfuls") also contains romantic fiction.

Although manuscript collections for individual authors are mentioned in Chapter 2 by individual author, the Boston University Mugar Memorial Library Special Collections should be especially noted. For several years, under the direction of Howard Gotlieb, the Mugar Library has been aggressively collecting the papers and manuscripts of twentieth-century authors. They have been successful partly because they have not been condescending toward writers of popular fiction. They also have an uncatalogued collection of books by the authors whose papers they hold. This collection is a particularly good source for out-of-print books if the Library of Congress does not have them or if Boston is closer to the researcher. For example, the Mugar Library has manuscripts and typescripts for about twelve of Dorothy Eden's novels, materials relating to Norah Lofts's *The Lost Queen*, manuscripts and books by the

romantic mystery writer Martha Albrand, books and typescripts by the historical
novelist Jan Westcott, materials relating to Finis Farr's biography of Margaret
Mitchell, 49 boxes of material relating to Catherine Cookson, 8 boxes on
Margaret S. Bannister, 110 boxes on Margaret Culkin Banning, manuscripts and
letters of Faith Baldwin, manuscripts of Barbara Cartland, and materials on
Mary Elgin.

But most interesting are materials on Anya Seton, Phyllis Whitney, and Michael
Avallone. Although there is only one box of Seton material, it is biographical;
the correspondence is especially fascinating. Michael Avallone is probably the
most successful of the gothic writers that so annoy Phyllis Whitney—men who
write under multiple female pseudonyms for paperback publishers. Avallone's
career has been prolific and highly successful, and this collection may be the
only way to pin down his career and pseudonyms. It includes manuscripts,
typescripts, letters, publicity, programs from dinners of the Mystery Writers
of America, and other items. The large Phyllis Whitney collection is probably
the most useful, since it reveals so clearly her method of writing described in
her book, *Writing Juvenile Stories and Novels*. There are many early manuscripts
from the period before she began to publish, correspondence with literary
agents between 1931 and 1937, other correspondence since 1940, newsclippings,
some books in translation, and a large file of correspondence about specific
books in progress between Whitney and her literary agent-editor, Patricia
Schartle. The Boston University Collection is a rich one, but a researcher may
not quote from the material without permission of the author.

BIBLIOGRAPHY

Ash, Lee. *Subject Collections: A Guide to Special Book Collections and Subject
    Emphases as Reported by University, College, Public, and Special Libraries
    and Museums in the United States and Canada.* 4th ed., rev. and enl.
    New York: R. R. Bowker, 1974.

———, and Denis Lorenz. *Subject Collections: A Guide to Special Book Collections
    and Subject Emphases as Reported by University, College, Public, and Special
    Libraries in the United States and Canada.* 3d ed., rev. and enl. New York:
    R. R. Bowker, 1967.

Black, Robert Kerr. *The Sadleir-Black Gothic Collection: An Address Before the
    Bibliographical Society of the University of Virgina, University of Virginia
    Library, 1949.* Charlottesville, Va.: University of Virginia Press, 1949.

Bragin, Charles. *Bibliography: Dime Novels, 1860-1964.* Rev. ed. Brooklyn, N.Y.:
    Dime Novel Club, 1964.

Dickson, Sarah Augusta. *Arents Collection.* New York: New York Public Library, 1957.

Leisy, Ernest E. *The American Historical Novel.* Norman, Okla.: University
    of Oklahoma Press, 1950.

New York Public Library. *Dictionary Catalog of the Henry W. and Albert
    A. Berg Collection of English and American Literature.* 5 vols. Boston:
    G. K. Hall, 1969.

_____. *Dictionary Catalog of the Rare Book Division*. Boston: G. K. Hall, 1971-.

_____, Manuscript Division. *Dictionary Catalog*. 2 vols. Boston: G. K. Hall, 1967.

Noel, Mary. *Villains Galore: The Heyday of the Popular Story Weekly*. New York: Macmillan, 1954.

O'Neil, Perry. Supplement to *Arents Collection*, by Sarah Augusta Dickinson. New York: New York Public Library, 1964.

Overbury, Bertha Van Riper. "Collecting American Women Authors." *Barnard Alumnae* 62 (Spring 1973): 4-5.

"The Overbury Collection of American Women." *Barnard Alumnae* 62 (Spring 1973): 2-3.

Smith, Warren Hunting. "Recent Acquisitions in Gothic Fiction." *Yale University Library Gazette* 8 (1934): 109-11.

Whitney, Phyllis A. *Writing Juvenile Stories and Novels*. Boston: The Writer, 1976.

Wright, Lyle H. *American Fiction, 1774-1850*. 1939. Rev. ed. San Marino, Calif.: Huntington Library Publications, 1969.

_____. *American Fiction, 1774-1900*. Louisville, Ky.: Lost Cause Press, 1970.

Wright, R. Glenn, comp. *Author Bibliography of English Language Fiction in the Library of Congress Through 1950*. Boston: G. K. Hall, 1973.

_____. *Chronological Bibliography of English Language Fiction in the Library of Congress Through 1950*. Boston: G. K. Hall, 1974.

_____. *Title Bibliography of English Language Fiction in the Library of Congress Through 1950*. Boston: G. K. Hall, 1976.

APPENDIX 2

Selected Chronology

1740-41   Samuel Richardson, *Pamela*
1747-48   Samuel Richardson, *Clarissa Harlowe*
1764   Horace Walpole, *The Castle of Otranto*
1791   Susanna Haswell Rowson, *Charlotte Temple: A Tale of Truth*
1794   Ann Radcliffe, *The Mysteries of Udolpho*
1796   Matthew Gregory Lewis, *The Monk*
1797   Hannah Webster Foster, *The Coquette*
1798   Anonymous, *Amelia; or, The Faithless Briton*
      Charles Brockden Brown, *Wieland*
1799   Helena Wells, *The Step-Mother*
      Charles Brockden Brown, *Ormond* and *Edgar Huntly*
1800   Anonymous, *The Female American*
      Sally Wood, *Julia; or, The Illuminated Baron*
1801   Tabitha Gilman Tenney, *Female Quixotism: Exhibited in the Romantic Opinions and Extravagant Adventures of Dorcasina Sheldon*
      Sally Wood, *Dorval; or, The Speculator*
1803   A Lady of Philadelphia (Martha Read?), *Monima; or, The Beggar Girl*
      Eliza Vicery, *Emily Hamilton*
1804   "A Lady of the State of New York, author of *Henry Villers*," *Moreland Vale; or, The Fair Fugitive*
1807   P. D. Manvill, *Lucinda, the Mountain Mourner*
1809   A Lady of Philadelphia, *Laura*
1811   Isaac Mitchell, *The Asylum; or, Alonzo and Melissa*
1813   Jane Austen, *Pride and Prejudice*
1814   Lucy Brewer, *The Female Marine*

1818   Jane Austen, *Northanger Abbey*
1822   Catharine Maria Sedgwick, *A New England Tale*
1824   Margaret Bayard Smith, *A Winter in Washington*
        Catharine Maria Sedgwick, *Redwood*
        Eliza Lanesford Foster Cushing, *Saratoga*
        Lydia Maria Francis Child, *Hobomok: A Tale of Early Times*
        Harriet Vaughn Foster Cheney, *A Peep at the Pilgrims in Sixteen
            Hundred Thirty-Six*
1825   Lydia Maria Francis Child, *The Rebels; or, Boston Before the Revolution*
1827   Harriet Vaughn Foster Cheney, *The Rivals of Acadia*
        Catharine Maria Sedgwick, *Hope Leslie*
1828   Susanna Haswell Rowson, *Lucy Temple; or, Charlotte's Daughter*
1830   Catharine Maria Sedgwick, *Clarence*
1836   Maria Monk, *Awful Disclosures*
1838   Elizabeth Oakes Smith, *Riches Without Wings*
1843   Maria Jane McIntosh, *Woman, an Enigma*
1844   George Lippard, *The Quaker City; or, The Monks of Monks Hall*
1846   Maria Jane McIntosh, *Two Lives*
1847   E. D. E. N. Southworth, *Retribution*
        Charlotte Brontë, *Jane Eyre*
1848   Eliza B. Lee, *Naomi*
1850   Nathaniel Hawthorne, *The Scarlet Letter*
        Caroline Lee Hentz, *Linda*
1851   E. D. E. N. Southworth, *Shannondale*
        Susan Warner (pseud., Elizabeth Wetherell), *The Wide, Wide World*
1852   E. D. E. N. Southworth, *The Curse of Clifton*
        Susan Warner, *Queechy*
1854   Mary Jane Holmes, *Tempest and Sunshine*
        Maria Susanna Cummins, *The Lamplighter*
        Marion Harland, *Alone*
        Ann Sophia Stephens, *Fashion and Famine*
        E. D. E. N. Southworth, *The Lost Heiress*
1855   E. D. E. N. Southworth, *The Deserted Wife*
1856   Mary Jane Holmes, *Lena Rivers* and *The Homestead on the Hillside*
        Caroline Lee Hentz, *Ernest Linwood*
        Caroline Chesebro', *Victoria; or, The World Overcome*
1857   Mary Jane Holmes, *Meadowbrook*
        Ann Sophia Stephens, *The Heiress of Greenhurst*
        Maria Susanna Cummins, *Mabel Vaughn*
        Catharine Maria Sedgwick, *Married or Single?*
1859   E. D. E. N. Southworth, *The Hidden Hand*
        Augusta Jane Evans Wilson, *Beulah*
1860   Ann Sophia Stephens, *Malaeska*
1863   E. D. E. N. Southworth, *The Fatal Marriage*
1866   H. B. Goodwin, *Sherbrooke*

1867   Augusta Jane Evans Wilson, *St. Elmo*
1872   Harriet Prescott Spofford, *A Thief in the Night*
1876   E. D. E. N. Southworth, *Self-Raised*
1882   Constance Fenimore Woolson, *Anne*
1884   Helen Hunt Jackson, *Ramona*
1898   Henry James, *The Turn of the Screw*
1900   Mary Johnston, *To Have and To Hold*
1911   Kathleen Norris, *Mother*
1912   Jean Webster, *Daddy-Long-Legs*
1919   Mary Roberts Rinehart, *Dangerous Days*
1921   Edith M. Hull, *The Sheik*
1930   Kathleen Norris, *The Love of Julie Borel*
1932   Kathleen Norris, *Wife for Sale*
        Francis Iles, *Before the Fact*
1935   Faith Baldwin, *Private Duty*
        Georgette Heyer, *Regency Buck*
1936   Margaret Mitchell, *Gone With the Wind*
        Daphne du Maurier, *Jamaica Inn*
1938   Daphne du Maurier, *Rebecca*
        Emilie Loring, *High of Heart*
1940   Grace Livingston Hill, *Rose Galbraith*
        Emilie Loring, *There Is Always Love*
1941   Anya Seton, *My Theodosia*
1942   Marcia Davenport, *Valley of Decision*
        Kathleen Norris, *Come Back to Me, Beloved*
1944   Kathleen Winsor, *Forever Amber*
        Anya Seton, *Dragonwyck*
        Elizabeth Goudge, *Green Dolphin Street*
1946   Emilie Loring, *Bright Skies*
1948   Jean Plaidy, *Beyond the Blue Mountains*
1950   Georgette Heyer, *The Grand Sophy*
1954   Anya Seton, *Katherine*
1955   Mary Stewart, *Madam, Will You Talk?*
        Phyllis Whitney, *The Quicksilver Pool*
1957   Georgette Heyer, *Sylvester; or, The Wicked Uncle*
1958   Anya Seton, *The Winthrop Woman*
        Mary Stewart, *Nine Coaches Waiting*
1959   Mary Stewart, *My Brother Michael*
1960   Victoria Holt, *Mistress of Mellyn*
1961   Georgette Heyer, *A Civil Contract*
1962   Anya Seton, *Devil Water*
        Mary Stewart, *The Moonspinners*
1963   Victoria Holt, *Bride of Pendorric*
1964   Dorothy Eden, *Ravenscroft*
        Mary Stewart, *This Rough Magic*

Phyllis Whitney, *Black Amber*
1965   Anya Seton, *Avalon*
1966   Victoria Holt, *Menfreya in the Morning*
        Phyllis Whitney, *Columbella*
        Emilie Loring, *Spring Always Comes*
1968   Phyllis Whitney, *Hunter's Green*
        Margaret Widdemer, *The Red Castle Women*
1970   Anne Hebert, *Kamouraska*
        Dorothy Eden, *Winterwood*
        Phyllis Whitney, *Lost Island*
1971   Susan Howatch, *Penmarric*
1972   Anya Seton, *Green Darkness*
        Kathleen Woodiwiss, *The Flame and the Flower*
1974   Susan Howatch, *Cashelmara*
        Lolah Burford, *MacLyon*
1976   Rosemary Rogers, *Wicked, Loving Lies*
        Mary Stewart, *Touch Not the Cat*
1977   Lolah Burford, *Alyx*
        Kathleen Woodiwiss, *Shanna*
1978   Phyllis Whitney, *The Glass Flame*
1979   Norah Lofts, *The Day of the Butterfly*
        Phyllis Whitney, *Domino*
        Victoria Holt, *The Spring of the Tiger*
1980   Phyllis Whitney, *Poinciana*
        Victoria Holt, *The Mask of the Enchantress*

Index

About the Author

Kay Mussell is Associate Professor of Literature and American Studies and Director of the American Studies Program at American University in Washington, D.C. Her articles have appeared in the *Journal of Popular Culture* and her contribution will appear in *The Female Gothic* (edited by Juliann E. Fleenor and Beth Greenfeld, forthcoming).